GIVING AND RECEIVING

GIVING AND RECEIVING

Morris Cerullo

Published for MCWE by Battle Books, an imprint of Hatpin Communications Ltd. 1, Station Road, Robertsbridge, East Sussex, TN32 5DE, Britain. Produced and printed by Nuprint Ltd., Station Road, Harpenden, Herts, AL5 4SE, Britain.

CONTENTS

Notes on reading the Bible

In this book there are many quotations from the Bible.

The Bible is divided into 'books' with 'chapters', and the chapters have 'verses'.

Sometimes a reference is made to a particular Bible passage – e.g. Isaiah 53:5-6.

To find this passage, check the index at the front of your Bible to see where the book of Isaiah can be found.

Next you want chapter 53 in Isaiah.

Finally you turn up verses 5 to 6 in chapter 53.

You may also want to read the verses immediately in front and even afterwards, to get a clearer understanding, and to ensure that the verses have not been quoted obviously out of context.

You can read this book without a Bible, but having one to hand could make all the difference.

FOREWORD

This is a simple book, written in plain English, for ordinary people. I've written it for three main reasons. Firstly, to provide some teaching on what is one of the most crucial issues of our day. Secondly, to respond to some of those critics who've suggested that I place too great a stress on giving. And thirdly, because I want all my partners to receive the joy and blessings which come from giving in God's way.

The work that I've done in over a hundred countries, preaching to millions of people and training hundreds of thousands of national leaders, has only been possible because of the committed, sacrificial giving by the believers who stand in partnership with me.

Their giving has borne enormous fruit, right around the world. But most of these givers will not see this fruit before they reach heaven. I hope that this book will help them to appreciate the deep spiritual significance of their giving, and that it will give them a small insight into the fabulous rewards which await them in heaven.

I'm sure you already know that God loves cheerful givers. And most of my partners know that God blesses givers. This book should help you to understand *why* he loves them so much and what you can do to become one.

It's also an intensely practical book, because I don't want you merely to know *about* giving and receiving – I want you to *become* a joyful generous giver.

You'd better not start reading this book if you want to hang on to all your earthly wealth. But, if you'd like to join the blessed and cheerful company of givers like Zacchaeus, then this is undoubtedly the book for you!

Please join me now, as we examine the words of the Bible. Put aside your preconceived ideas about giving. Move away from the shifting sands of your tradition and personal experience. Prepare to excavate the solid rock of Scripture.

Get ready to become a cheerful giver and to start receiving God's special blessings.

Morris Cerullo
June 1995

INTRODUCTION

Many different controversies have swept the church in the forty-five years that I've been ministering. There have been disputes about miracles, debates on baptism in the Spirit, arguments over Endtimes, disagreements about shepherding, and discussions on the place of ordinary people in ministry.

However, the current controversy is all about giving. I know that critics have always accused the church of being too interested in money. But, right now, wherever I go in the world, people pump me with questions about financial principles – especially giving. And that's exactly as it should be, for the Bible records Jesus teaching more about money than any other topic – even more than about prayer.

We live in an age of tremendous financial instability – with rising debts, regular economic crises, and a world-wide increase in unemployment, homelessness and begging. Quite naturally, people wonder how it can be right or wise to give money away in times like these.

Sometimes it seems that debt grips the entire world. Massive international debts have paralyzed whole nations in Africa, Eastern Europe and Latin America. And easy credit,

9

expensive house purchases and long-lasting recession have pushed large numbers of North American and Western European families into a form of financial imprisonment.

These national and personal debts may seem inescapable, and giving doesn't appear to be the obvious way out. Many wonder whether God is relevant to their financial need. Some, in desperation, do pray for divine help. However, nearly all neglect to search the Bible for a solution to their problems. Yet the answers are there – plain for all to read.

International financial crises seem to influence our affairs more than ever. But despite all the talk, the problems only get worse. Inflation is out-of-control in too many countries. World-wide unemployment is at record levels. Unfair competition cripples Third World nations. And some large corporations exploit the poor to make extortionate profits.

Difficult times

Faced with times like these, it's little wonder that most people prefer to keep what money they have rather than give it away to others.

Yet that's what I urge people to do, for I earnestly believe that giving is vital to our spiritual health. If we are children of the God who 'so loved the world that he gave', then surely his sacrificial giving should be central to our lives.

Some people are always looking for excuses to dilute God's word or to explain away Jesus' teaching. They wonder how relevant his financial instructions can be today. Is it really wise, they ask, to 'give to everyone who asks' when there are so many con-men after our money?

Yet Jesus taught in difficult times. He lived when taxes were at record levels, multitudes begged by the roadside, and people were regularly cheated by government officials.

Today however, on top of these sorts of personal demands, we also receive many impersonal requests for donations from charities and Christian ministries. They appeal for funds in letters, over the phone and on television. But though we may face more claims on our giving than earlier generations, the basic divine principle still remains the same. God really does love a cheerful giver.

Recent controversies

In the last twenty years, Christian arguments about giving have focused on three main issues. Firstly, people have wondered whether they should tithe their income. (Tithe is an old word for 10%.) Some teachers maintain that the Old Testament practice of tithing is not God's pattern for today. They argue that tithing is rarely mentioned in the New Testament and is too 'legalistic' for the Age of Grace.

Other ministers insist that tithing is a basic Biblical practice – like prayer and fasting – which is right for all time. They say that it develops self-discipline and faith, and is vital for the financial health of the church. In this book, I'm going to set out all the Bible teaching on tithing. By the end, we should be able to make up our minds about this issue.

Secondly, people have argued about who should receive the tithe or main gift. Most pastors say that believers should give the tithe or largest portion to their local church. A few leaders insist that *all* their members' giving should go to the local church. Many Christian societies argue that believers should listen to God and give as he directs. And then there are those who believe that Christian giving should be directed mainly towards the poor and needy.

I'm going to show what the Bible teaches on this important issue. When we reach the last page, we'll know what God wants us to do with our money.

Thirdly, people have debated the issue of 'prosperity'. This is the controversy about what happens to givers after they've given. Some teachers argue that God *automatically* blesses all those who give in a way which brings 'health and wealth' in proportion to the size of their gift.

Other church leaders challenge this idea. They say that truly biblical giving is sacrificial, and that this means givers will *usually* have less after giving. These leaders agree that God blesses givers spiritually. However, they reject the idea that God *always* rewards givers with material prosperity.

In this book, I'll point out what the Bible teaches about receiving, so that we can know what blessings to expect in our earthly lives as a result of our generous giving.

The basic question

Although many ministers are fascinated by these three issues, most ordinary believers are concerned with a more basic question. They want to know *why* they should give.

Questions like 'How much?' 'To whom?' and 'What happens?' will only seriously interest us when we're convinced that we should give. Or, better still, when we're consumed with a love which compels us to give.

As we go through the Biblical teaching on giving, I'll point out *why* people gave in the Scriptures. We'll see a variety of reasons – some good, some bad, some selfish, some selfless. Among these we'll find God's reason for giving, which surely is the motive we should aim for ourselves.

Although we will learn from generous people, we'll look more closely at the giving God. As forgiven believers, we are God's children and servants. We know that we should be like God, and – day by day – the Holy Spirit is making us more like him. This means that we should want God's pattern of giving, not human ideas, to shape our giving.

Spiritual and financial gifts

In the last thirty years, there has been a tremendous growth in 'spiritual gifts'. Most Christian groups have received and developed different gifts of the Spirit. Countless books and conferences have focused on 'the gifts'. Yet few leaders have integrated their understanding of spiritual gifts with their thinking about financial giving.

Our God is the all-giving God, and it's foolish to divide his gifts between different boxes. So it is with our 'theology' of giving. Christian leaders – especially those, like me, who are 'pentecostal' and 'charismatic' – ought to realize that their ideas about 'gifts' should relate to their teaching on giving.

We emphasize the need to receive spiritual gifts from God. We urge people to use these gifts to benefit others and build up the church. So surely it makes sense also to encourage folk to receive material gifts from God – and to use them to assist others and advance the church.

This is a book about being greatly blessed and very cheerful givers. In it, I try to set out the biblical teaching on giving and receiving. I deal mainly with the way that we give finance. However, please remember that giving is a much bigger topic than money alone.

More than money

Page by page, I'll show that God wants us to give like him. But he doesn't want us to give just our money. He wants generosity to dominate *every* area of our lives.

We are supposed to be all-giving Christians. People who are ready to give spiritual help to everyone. Believers who are keen to share the 'Good News' with people around us. Disciples who are eager to pass on God's words and God's gifts to build Christ's church and extend God's kingdom.

We know that we are called to develop our skills and

abilities, not to bury them. These natural talents from God are meant to be used – to be given away – to benefit others.

We recognize that the Bible urges us to practise hospitality. A Christian home should be a welcoming oasis, not a closed castle. It should be used for others – especially the poor and strangers. Our homes, our food, our furniture, our clothes, our cars, our possessions – all these have been given to us by our heavenly Father. And we are called to use them as generously as God.

Sometimes it seems easier to give a small sum of 'conscious' money, than to make time to help a needy person. But God wants us to be people who delight to give the precious gift of our time and attention. Kind words and deeds are often more valuable than hard cash – and so the gift of time is as important as the gift of money.

But most of all, God wants us to give our love. He gave his Son because he 'so loved the world'. His gift of Jesus was not only motivated by love, it was itself a gift of love. And so we, made in God's image, are called to give our love to the world with equal generosity – even to our enemies.

We are about to go on a journey together through the Scriptures. We are going to gaze at the all-giving God, and learn from him how we should give. We will study stories in the lives of some scriptural heroes – plus one or two rogues – to benefit from their examples.

And we will carefully examine Jesus' words about giving and receiving. Our intention is to obey them, because we know that they are truth – the way to abundant life.

THE GIVING GOD

When we think about God and try to find a word to describe him, we don't often come up with 'giving'. We're more familiar with God being called 'loving', 'forgiving', 'just', 'gracious', 'merciful' and so on. But it's time to realize that 'giving' is at the heart of all these divine characteristics.

Love is something that we give to others – we can't keep it back for ourselves. Grace is the technical word for God's freely given, undeserved favour. The link between forgiveness and giving is obvious, though often overlooked. Justice and mercy, like love, can only be given freely.

Please remember, that if a condition could be attached to grace, it would no longer be essentially gracious. Wherever justice and love are 'for sale', they are corrupt and false. It's the same with forgiveness and mercy – when they are not given freely they aren't the genuine article.

Our God is a genuine giver – through and through. Everything we know about him reveals his lavish divine generosity. Examples of his giving surround us all. Our homes, our families, our abilities, our life, our world – these all reveal the generous nature of our all-giving God.

When Jesus was talking to the people in Matthew 7:11, he said this. 'If you then, who are evil, know how to give good gifts to your children, how much more will your Father who is in heaven give good things to those who ask him!'

Jesus reminded the people that God was their Father. Like all fathers, he said, God loves to bless his children with gifts. Then Jesus pointed out that – unlike human fathers – God is not evil. God's generosity to his children is far greater than that which we see in ourselves or our parents.

> If you who are evil know how to give good gifts to your children, how much more will your Father in heaven give good things to those who ask him.

The Bible describes God in two important ways which summarize his generosity. It names him as 'Creator' and as 'Redeemer'. God is the one who gives us material life and the one who gives us spiritual life! These titles reveal the essence of God – and throughout the Bible he is worshipped in *both* these roles.

In Revelation 4:11, the elders sang, 'Worthy are you, our Lord and God, to receive glory and honour and power, for you created all things, and by your will they existed and were created'. A few verses later in 5:9, they sang: 'Worthy are you to take the scroll and to open its seals, for you were slain and by your blood did ransom men for God'.

The Bible celebrates God's twin gifts of creation and redemption – his material giving and his spiritual giving. The scriptures don't suggest that his spiritual gifts are more important than his material gifts, or vice versa – both are appreciated with equal enthusiasm.

We see this clearly in Colossians 1:15-20. This is a short hymn which praises Christ as head of creation. The first verse acclaims him because 'in him all things were created', and the second for 'making peace by the blood of his cross'.

The Creator's Gift

The Bible begins with God's gift of creation. Genesis opens with a marvelous description of our world's origin. Timeless words introduce us to our God. 'In the beginning God created the heavens and the earth.' He is the Creator.

Christians may disagree over some of the details about creation, but the basic principle is plain. One God existed before the world, and everything came forth from nothing at his command. However, it's important to realize that creation was not a divine whim; it was the first gift.

THE GIFT OF LIFE

Genesis 1:29 records God's first words to men and women – 'Behold I have given you...'. These words are often overlooked, but they reveal God's nature right at the outset of his relationship with humanity. He is a giver, and creation is his gift to us, to all people everywhere.

Most of the time, we take our lives and environment for granted. We may value 'life' when we have a near-miss in a car or have just recovered from a serious illness, but we rarely give thanks to God for his gift of life.

Behold I have given you...

However, the book of Psalms is packed with songs which express the Jews' gratitude for God's gift of creation.

Psalm 19 begins with 'The heavens are telling the glory of God; and the firmament proclaims his handiwork'. (See how it moves from material to spiritual in verse seven, and ends by describing God as, 'My rock and my redeemer'.)

Universal life

Psalm 104 is, perhaps, the greatest Jewish celebration of God's gift of life. Read it now and see how it takes us on a wonderful guided tour of creation. Truly, as verse twenty-five states, 'O Lord, how manifold are your works!'

Hundreds of millions of people now live in cities and – as a result – have little personal contact with creation. They rarely see creatures and countryside, mountains and oceans. Instead of being able to enjoy God's free gifts, city-dwellers often have to spend their time and money on costly man-made amusements.

The New Age movement loves the creator's gift, but rejects the Creator

Yet television documentaries have introduced us to far more of the world's wonders than our ancestors ever knew. And, although our experience is usually 'second-hand', people are increasingly concerned with the environment.

The 'New Age' movement loves the creator's gift, but rejects the Creator. Science and astronomy have opened our eyes to the vastness and complexity of creation. Yet most people now value life while they disregard the giver of life. Isn't it time for us – as believing children of the Creator – to set an example to the world? Shouldn't we give more time to enjoying his gift of life *and* expressing our gratitude in praise, worship and daily adoration?

The world's selfish materialism will seem the best way to behave when nearly all our activities cost money and we're charged for virtually everything we do. If we're familiar with paying for things, it'll seem right to charge rather than to give – or to expect some sort of return when we do give.

However, our attitude will start to change when we soak ourselves in the gift of creation. God's amazing generosity will begin to infect us when we finally grasp the truth that the world's natural beauty is an amazing free gift to us all.

Giving soon becomes second-nature to those who live in an environment of endless generosity. Which, of course, is exactly where we Christians do live – all the time!

Personal life

God created everything in the world and gave it to us all for our enjoyment and care. But he also made us as unique individuals. He made me and he made you: he's personally given us our very own existence.

Once again, the Psalms include many hymns which praise God for this gift of personal life. Psalm 139 is well known. 'It was you who created my inmost self, and put me together in my mother's womb; for all these mysteries I thank you: for the wonder of myself, for the wonder of your works.'

Sometimes we're pleased with our own achievements. We boast of what we've done. Maybe occasionally we remember to thank our parents for their contribution to our existence, but how often do we acknowledge that the hand of God is directly behind them?

Our minds and bodies, our size and intellects, our families and race, even our breath – all these are personal gifts. Remember, God doesn't love us because we're part of the world. He loves the world because it's full of people like us whom he loves personally, passionately and uniquely.

> You created my inmost self, and put me together in my mother's womb; for all these mysteries I thank you

EXTRAVAGANT GIVING

When we think about God as creator, we quickly see the extravagance of his giving. A universe which is ridiculously large, with gigantic galaxies spiraling out of sight. A lush planet which is teeming with life, packed with an enormous variety of plants and creatures. Time and again, God's people have had to admit the impossibility of counting the stars in the sky and the grains of sand on the seashore.

Enormous variety

The story of Noah's Ark highlights the diversity which is typical of the creator's giving. A massive liner was needed to preserve a sample of all the known species. Whenever God gives, whatever he gives, there is seemingly endless variety – animals, plants, climate, scenery and so on. Why are there so many species of birds and insects? Why is every snowflake and fingerprint unique? Why are there so many differences between individuals? It's because God is such an incredibly extravagant giver.

> Whenever God gives, whatever he gives, there is seemingly endless variety

Psalms 104 and 148 describe the variety of creation and naturally climax in pleas to 'Praise the Lord'. The extraordinary variety of creation shouts a message about God. His handiwork tells us something about himself. It's not only that he is a generous giver, it's also that his giving is creative and varied.

That's a vital lesson for us today!

Non-stop extravagance

When people think about God as Creator, they can fall into the trap of assuming that his creative work ended in Eden. But God's extravagant giving in creation is continuous. Lamentations 3:22-23 promises that, 'The steadfast love of the Lord *never* ceases, his mercies never come to an end, they are new *every* morning'.

Psalm 104 moves between what God *did* at creation and what he *still does* for creation. Verses 27-29 show that creation's continued existence depends on the Creator's extravagant non-stop giving. And verse 30 makes it clear that God's creative giving is still relevant: 'When you send forth your Spirit, they *are* created'.

We are drawing very near to God's final creative act. Every day brings Revelation 21:5 closer, when God has promised to make, 'the whole of creation new'. It's revealing that, in Revelation 21:6, God then says, 'I am the Beginning and the End. *I will give* water from the well of life *free* to anybody who is thirsty'.

We have already seen that the Bible begins with God promising men and women, 'I give you'. Here we see that the Scriptures end with God guaranteeing yet another free gift. Truly our Creator is the Great Non-Stop Giver.

RISKY GIVING

All true giving must carry some sort of risk. In fact, if there is no risk there's no gift. A gift cannot be considered a real gift if it's given with strict conditions which must be obeyed – or the gift will be snatched back by the giver. Equally, a gift is not genuine if the giver is entirely uninterested in what happens to it.

When we give a present to a friend, we have no control over what they do with it. We may hope that our present will be valued and useful. But we'll know there's a chance that it could be misused, ignored, forgotten or broken. That's the risk we take in giving. Even if we include clear instructions with our gift, we'll know that these – and the present itself – can be casually disregarded.

> Millions of people don't think of creation as a gift, and don't give a moment's thought to the giver

Taken for granted

So it is with God's gift to us of creation. There was always a risk that humanity would take it for granted. And that's exactly what's happened. Millions, billions of people don't think of creation as a gift, and don't give a moment's thought to the giver.

How does God feel about this? How do we feel when our carefully chosen gifts are ignored by someone we love? Does it cause God's love to decrease? Has he stopped giving out of irritation and anger? Of course not!

True giving doesn't think about the response and isn't motivated solely by the hope of something in return. If God gave just to get some sort of response from us, it wouldn't be selfless giving. He wouldn't be all-loving!

Corrupted

When God made the world and gave it to humanity, there was a risk that his gift would be abused, spoilt, broken, polluted, corrupted. That, too, is precisely what happened.

In Romans 8:18-22, Paul makes it clear that creation is not to blame for its corruption, and that – like us – it longs for divine transformation, for redemption. 'Creation itself will be set free from its bondage to decay and obtain the glorious liberty of the children of God. We know that the whole creation has been groaning in travail together until now...'

It gets easier every day for us to see the way that men and women have spoilt God's gift of creation. Pollution has highlighted humanity's selfish wickedness. It is our fault that this precious, awesome gift is being ruined. We – and the gift – need the Giver to save us and to renew the gift.

The Redeemer's Gift

Many Christians think more about God as redeemer than as creator. But remember, he's only a redeemer because he's a creator who gave extravagant gifts which have been misused and corrupted. The Bible worships God equally as Creator and Redeemer – and giving is basic to both actions.

In this chapter I'm trying to show that giving is fundamental to the character of God. I want us to grasp that God gives and he gives, and we go on receiving!

All Christianity's great doctrines are based on some aspect of God's giving. So we won't understand why and how we should give until we know for certain that we serve and follow the all-giving God.

> We won't understand why and how we should give until we know that we serve the all-giving God

The gift of creation may be incredibly wonderful, but we know that God's greatest gift of all is his only Son – especially the death of his Son.

THE GIFT OF SALVATION

The New Testament explains Christ's death in several different ways, using a variety of expressions. That's because one figure of speech can't provide a total understanding of what his death means.

In this section I'm not examining every detailed accomplishment of his glorious death. Instead I'm trying to show how the key phrases illustrate God's generosity.

Sacrifice

The New Testament writers often use sacrificial language to describe Christ's death. They do this to show three things.

Firstly, that Christ fulfilled all the Old Testament ritual which God had provided to help people approach him. Secondly, that all the Jewish ritual sacrifices had ended. And thirdly, that Christ was their substitute.

We'll inspect the ritual later to see what it teaches us about our giving. But here we're going to survey the biblical language which describes the greatest sacrifice of all.

Jesus is repeatedly called the slain lamb of God, whose precious blood takes away the sin of the world. We can read about this in John 1:29, 36; 1 Peter 1:18-19; and Revelation 5:6-10 & 13:8.

Paul describes Christ as the true Passover lamb in 1 Corinthians 5:6-8, and as a sin-offering in Romans 8:3. Ephesians 5:2 is probably his clearest description of sacrifice. 'Walk in love, as Christ loved us and gave himself up for us, a fragrant offering and sacrifice to God.'

This important verse reveals much about Paul's understanding of sacrifice. It offers no hint of sacrifice being a means of placating an angry God. Instead it shows that true sacrifice is always rooted in love and can never be reversed – because it's a complete giving up, a total release, of whatever is given.

Ephesians 5:2 brings out the idea that sacrifice – when it expresses best love – is immensely pleasing to God. And it shows that Christ's selfless giving should have a profound effect on the way we live.

In this verse, Paul tells us to walk in love because Christ loved us. He goes on to say that the best expression of this love is that he gave himself up for us as a sacrifice to God.

This is precisely why we're starting our study of giving by gazing at God. We're called to live as he lived, to love as he loved and to give as he gave. We won't know how to give until we've grasped the extent of God's giving.

The book of Hebrews is the New Testament textbook on the doctrine of Christ's sacrifice. Once again, in this book, I'm not examining the accomplishments of his death; rather I'm showing what they teach about God's giving.

Hebrews stresses the voluntary nature of Christ's sacrifice, contrasting it with the helpless victims of the Old Testament ritual. And it emphasizes that a sacrifice must be God's will if it's to be acceptable and pleasing to him.

Hebrews ends with some practical conclusions based in sacrifice, and with a prayer for sacrifice. 'Let us go forth and bear the abuse he endured (13:13).' 'Let us continually offer up a sacrifice of praise to God, the fruit of lips that acknowledge his name (13:15) 'Do not neglect to do good and to share what you have, for such sacrifices are pleasing to God (13:16) 'May God equip you with everything good that you may do his will, working in you that which is pleasing in his sight (vs. 21.'

> Do not neglect to do good and to share what you have, for such sacrifices are pleasing to God

These, and other New Testament passages, show conclusively that the sacrifice of Christ's death was a voluntary gift, of great love, at immense personal cost. It permanently dealt with our sin and made possible God's gift to us of forgiveness.

The use of the word 'sacrifice' dramatically underlined to first-century Jews the fact that God had given the best that he had, and that his giving was irreversible.

Redemption

This is another New Testament word-picture which meant something special to first century people. Today, redemption is thought of as a religious word. But then it was the everyday word which described paying a price to obtain somebody's release from an evil.

Prisoners of war might be released on payment of a fixed price called a 'ransom'. And slaves could be released by a ransom in one of two ways: either they paid their master the price of freedom or they were purchased by a 'god'.

In the last instance, a slave would pay his ransom money into the relevant temple treasury, and then be ceremoniously sold to that 'god'. Technically, he would always be the slave of that god and would have occasional duties to perform at the god's temple. But as far as people were concerned, he was a completely free man.

In all these everyday usages of the word 'redemption', it was the payment of the right price which mattered the most.

Jesus taught that whoever sinned was the slave of sin, and Paul often reminded his readers that they were – or had been – slaves of sin under sentence of death. Without redemption, their slavery would continue.

The New Testament writers seized upon this word-picture as a wonderful description for Christ's death because it was packed with meaning for the people of their day. So Christ's death was called 'a ransom for many' and redemption language is often used in the Scriptures.

What mattered was the payment of the right price

Titus 2:14 describes Jesus as one 'who gave himself for us to redeem us from all iniquity'. 1 Timothy 2:6 says that Christ 'gave himself as a ransom for all'. 1 Corinthians 6:19-20 specifies that we 'were bought with a price'.

Colossians 1:13-14 says that God 'has delivered us from the dominion of darkness and transferred us to the kingdom of his beloved Son, in whom we have redemption, the forgiveness of sins'.

Ephesians 1:7-8 uses similar words which underline God's extreme generosity. 'In him we have redemption through his blood, the forgiveness

> We have redemption through his blood according to the riches of his grace which he has lavished upon us

of our sins, according to the riches of his grace which he has lavished upon us.'

There are many other verses in the New Testament which use the picture of redemption to describe the Father's gift of his Son and the Son's self-giving. However it's not just a New Testament idea: Jews in the Old Testament also worshipped God as their Redeemer.

Exodus 6:6 and Psalms 77:15 speak of God redeeming his people 'with a stretched out arm'. Because God loved his people he redeemed them at cost to himself, and his great effort was regarded as the 'price'.

Just as we've seen that God's 'creating' did not end in Eden, so the New Testament also shows that God's 'redeeming' did not stop at Calvary: Ephesians 4:30 points us forward to a future day of Redemption.

The language of redemption is truly glorious. It makes plain that we've been redeemed from a great evil: we're slaves set free and prisoners of war who've been released. But more importantly for us in this book, it also reveals that God in his generosity was willing to pay an enormous price.

Payment is basic to the word-picture 'redemption'. So whenever God is worshipped as Redeemer we must realize that he is being praised as a great payer. The price he paid is the life, the blood, the death, of his only beloved Son. Don't forget, God didn't have to redeem us. But he did so at immense personal cost. Why? Because of his great love and because he's a generous giver by nature.

The New Testament also shows us that redemption – like

sacrifice – should have a profound effect on the way we live. 1 Corinthians 6:20 states, 'You were bought with a price. So glorify God in your body'.

Galatians goes further. In 3:13 we're told that Christ redeemed us from the curse of the law so that we might receive both the blessing of Abraham and the promise of the Spirit. Then in 5:1 we're urged not to submit again to slavery because Christ has set us free for freedom.

> When God gave *for* us in redemption, he didn't give to receive anything himself in return, but so that he could give *to* us more of his blessings

This shows that when God gave for us in redemption, he didn't give to receive anything himself in return. Instead he gave so that he could give to us even more of his blessings. That's the sort of giver he is! And that's the pattern of giving which we're called, as God's children, to follow.

Justification

The New Testament also uses this word-picture to describe the effects of Christ's death. 'Sacrifice' and 'redemption' reminded early believers of temple worship and slave markets, but 'justification' made them think of law courts.

'Justify' is a legal expression which means the opposite of 'condemn'. So when the Bible describes God as justifying sinners, it means that we are not condemned – we are acquitted by 'the Judge of all the earth'.

True Justice can never be bought. And because all humanity has sinned, we deserve nothing but condemnation from the universal judge. However, Paul makes it clear in Romans 3:23-24 that – even though we 'all have sinned and fall short of the glory of God' – we 'are justified by his grace as a gift'.

Once again, we see that it's all a free gift. There's nothing we can do to offset our sins, and there's nothing we can do to earn our acquittal. The all-giving God acknowledges our guilt, but he pardons those who are united with Christ as an incredible free gift.

> We are justified by his grace as a gift

Read Romans 5:15-21 and praise God!

Justification is one of the most misunderstood Christian doctrines and is often confused with other ideas. However, I'm not explaining the detailed achievements of Christ's death in this chapter, I'm merely pointing out that the Bible describes Calvary and its accomplishments in terms of 'gift'.

As with all God's giving, 'justification' is future as well as past. We don't only look back at God's gifts, we also look forward to them.

1 Corinthians 6:11 reflects: 'you were justified in the name of the Lord Jesus Christ and in the Spirit of our God'. Romans 8:33 speaks of the present: 'it is God who justifies'. And Romans 5:19 looks forward: 'by one man's obedience many will be made righteous'.

Justification means that the divine verdict 'guilty but pardoned', rather than 'guilty and condemned', has been declared. It is this conviction of pardon which forms the basis of our assurance as Christians.

Those of us who have accepted this gift by faith can go on to make one of two responses. The most obvious one is a life of thanksgiving. We can be so grateful for God's gift that we allow it to change us. That's the point of this book that – out of gratitude to God – we start to live and give like him.

> We don't only look back at God's gifts, we also look forward to them

The second response is a casual attitude to sin. In Romans 6:1, Paul recognizes that the assurance of acquittal may lead some people to be careless about sinning. He then quickly rejects this idea as unthinkable. Yet the lack of giving in the church surely suggests that many of today's Christians are not exactly overflowing with gratitude for their redemption – the greatest gift of all.

> The lack of giving in the church suggests that many of today's Christians are not overflowing with thanksgiving for their redemption

Reconciliation

For first-century people, this word-picture described the achievements of Christ's death in terms of human relationships. It was the word they used for ending hostilities, for finally bridging over a nasty long-lasting quarrel, for making peace at the end of a war.

Throughout the Bible, it's clear that sinners are the 'enemies' of God. And the New Testament makes it plain that God is vigorously opposed to everything evil. This means that it's impossible for people and God to have an intimate relationship without 'reconciliation'.

We all know that the way to mend a broken human relationship is to take away the cause of the quarrel and offer forgiveness. We can apologize for something we've said or done, pay any money that's due, make reparation or restitution as appropriate – and so on. In every case, the way to reconciliation lies through grappling effectively with the root cause of the enmity.

The Son died to put away our sin. As a result, the Father now offers to forgive us. Together they've made the way wide open for all people to come back to God. That's what is meant by reconciliation.

Romans 5:10 states that, 'while we were enemies we were reconciled to God by the death of his Son'. And both

Colossians 1:15-22 and Ephesians 2:1-22 make extensive use of the 'reconciliation' picture. Read them now and notice how they do this in passages which present God as a creator. Remember, it's the all-giving Creator who gives what is needed to make reconciliation possible.

Ephesians 2:14 shows that Christ 'is our peace, who has made us both one, and has broken down the dividing wall of hostility'. It then goes on to state that Christ did this so he 'might create in himself one new man in place of the two, so making peace, and might reconcile us both to God in one body through the cross, thereby bringing the hostility to an end'.

Reconciliation, like the other words we've looked at, should make a difference. 2 Corinthians 5:18 states, 'All this is from God, who through Christ reconciled us to himself and *gave us* the ministry of reconciliation'.

It's the all-giving Creator who gives what is needed to make reconciliation possible

We all know from everyday experience that gifts are a vital part of mending broken relationships. From a bunch of flowers after a domestic row right up to reparations after a war, giving is the medicine which heals human enmity.

Giving in human reconciliation works something like this. An offender offers a gift with sincere apologies to the person he's hurt. The one who's been hurt may then either accept the gift and offer sincere forgiveness, or turn their back on the offender and continue the enmity.

Christ offered his life on our behalf to the One who'd been hurt by our sin. God has accepted Christ's gift and has offered us the gift of forgiveness.

It's the gift of Christ's death which has made possible our reconciliation with God. Reconciliation without gifts is impossible because it's an action which just has to include giving. As God has given us the ministry of reconciliation, it's urgent that we start to become people who always give as generously and cheerfully as our God.

THE GIFT OF LOVE

Ephesians 2 is a vital chapter for any study of God's all-giving nature. Verses 4-10 summarize wonderfully the nature of the creating, redeeming God we worship.

'For God, who is rich in mercy, out of the great love with which he loved us, even when we were dead through our trespasses, made us alive together with Christ (by grace you have been saved), and raised us up with him, and made us sit with him in the heavenly places in Christ Jesus, that in the coming ages he might show the immeasurable riches of his grace in kindness towards us in Christ Jesus. For by grace you have been saved through faith; and this is not your own doing, it is the gift of God – not because of works, lest any man should boast. For we are his workmanship, created in Christ Jesus for good works, which God prepared beforehand, that we should walk in them.'

> **This is not your own doing, it is the gift of God**

These verses define God as rich in mercy. They show that he has great love for all those who are dead through their trespasses and sin. They demonstrate that our redemption is given so that God can then give us even more from his immeasurable riches of grace. And they prove that we have been redeemed with a purpose – for good works.

It's natural for people to give presents to those that they love. What's different about God is that his loving giving embraces all humanity – even those who are his enemies.

God doesn't restrict his love and giving to those who deserve it, to those who've earnt it, or to those who might give something back in return. In fact God is so rich in mercy that the Bible describes him as mercy full: mercy dominates and characterizes all God's activities.

Much Christian giving today is restricted and shaped by concerns which are absent in God's giving. People want to know whether the person or society is trustworthy, whether they'll make good use of the gift, whether they've a good track record. Thank God that he doesn't act like that or none of us would ever have received anything!

God is rich in mercy. He gives freely to all without any conditions. He gives as generously to the undeserving as to the righteous. And he does this because he is filled by enormous love for his corrupt and fallen creation.

> People want to know whether the person is trustworthy, whether they'll make good use of the gift, whether they've a good track record. Thank God he doesn't give like that!

Remember, God gives because he loves. No matter whether his gifts are spiritual or material, every one of them is an expression of his love. We'll never begin to give like him until we start to love like him. And we won't develop in our God-given ministry of reconciliation until selfless love is our strongest motive for giving anything and everything.

There's a job for us to do. We're to be reconcilers – ambassadors for Christ – urging people to be reconciled to God. And we've seen that this involves giving like God. We're to do good by sharing what we have – and now we know that this means sacrifice.

Most important of all, we're to walk in love because Christ loved us. We're called to care so much for the physical and spiritual condition of others that we give and give and go on giving – of ourselves and from our resources.

A few people have suggested that I over-emphasize

giving. But, the only question there should be about giving is why we give so little in response to God's enormous love.

I think that those who urge caution in giving should join us in gazing at the man on the cross. Perhaps then they'll start to express more gratitude for his extravagant love.

God is our standard. Christ is our example. Calvary is our pattern. Our creator and redeemer has given everything for us. Let us – in gratitude for what we have received from him – now become givers like him.

GIVING IN ISRAEL

In this chapter, I want to show the level of giving that God demanded from Israel in the days of the Old Testament. If we're to appreciate the degree of generosity which God expects today in his church, we must grasp the principles that he laid down so long ago. In the next chapter, we'll learn from incidents in the lives of Old Testament people. But here we're returning to God's first rules of giving.

There were three areas of giving for the children of Israel. They gave (1) sacrifices to God, (2) tithes to the poor and religious leaders, (3) freewill offerings for special projects. We'll look at these areas in turn to discover the principles involved – not to examine the details.

SACRIFICES

Sacrifices were gifts given directly to God. Cain and Abel's gifts are the first sacrifices offered to God in the Bible. As we'll see in the next chapter, patriarchs like Abraham, Isaac and Jacob also honored and thanked God by sacrifices. However, it was Moses who laid down God's laws about sacrifices for the Jews. These regulations are scattered throughout Exodus, Leviticus, Numbers and Deuteronomy.

The first seven chapters of Leviticus are the most important section of all.

There were five types of sacrifice, all with different details and purposes. I'm not going to describe them here as we're concerned only with the principles behind all sacrifices.

What was sacrificed

There were two basic principles. First, every sacrifice had to come from the personal property of the worshipper – animals, crops or kitchen produce were acceptable.

Every sacrifice had to come from the personal property of the worshipper

People could catch fish and wild animals and eat these themselves, but they could not offer them to God. Wild animals were thought to belong to God already, whereas domestic animals were deemed to be the worshipper's personal property.

The Jews could not offer God in sacrifice anything which they had unlawfully obtained. Only goods which had been produced by 'the sweat of his brow' were acceptable.

The second principle was that only the best would do for God. The offering had to be 'without blemish'. Physically perfect, mature, male animals were the preferred sacrifices.

The poor were allowed to offer God less valuable animals like doves, but these still had to be the best available

Only the best would do for God

specimens. If even a dove was too much, they could make an offering of cereals – but it had to be the best they had.

The people couldn't keep back the best of their property for themselves – offering God their cast-offs, left-overs and rubbish. Instead, they willingly gave him their best, and that's the principle we're called to follow.

When sacrifices were made

The five types of ritual sacrifice laid down by Moses were all made on a wide variety of occasions. They were offered personally and nationally, privately and publicly, regularly and as special needs arose. Numbers 28-29 gives a full list of the daily, weekly, monthly and annual public sacrifices. Exodus 12 shows how the Passover was celebrated privately within the family unit.

In Israel, no matter what the reason, whenever the people turned to God they worshipped him by offering him sacrifices. Sometimes we think today that the Jews only offered sacrifices to deal with their sin. But the Bible shows that they gave sacrificially to God when they rejoiced as well as when they wept. Sacrifices were offered to seal a vow (2 Samuel 15:7-9) and to release a man from a vow (Numbers 6). They were spontaneous acts of worship (Judges 13:17-23). They marked the purification of a woman after childbirth, and of lepers (Leviticus 12 & 14). They featured at the ordination of a priest, and at the offering of a Levite to God (Leviticus 8 & Numbers 8). They were offered at times of national repentance and imminent battle (1 Samuel 7 & 13:8-12). And they were central to royal coronations and the dedication of sanctuaries (1 Kings 1:9-12 & 8:1-13).

> No matter what the reason, whenever the people turned to God they worshipped him by offering him sacrifices

Two of the five types of sacrifice (the communion and the holocaust) were used for all the purposes we've just seen, but particularly for celebrating, thanking and consecrating. The other three types (cereal, sin and guilt offerings) had a different purpose: they temporarily covered the worshippers' sins and canceled their guilt.

Why sacrifices were made

Holocaust and communion sacrifices helped people express their feelings of being creatures who belonged to God. The holocaust represented the dedication of everything that the worshipper had and was. The communion – which was eaten together by the priest and the worshipper – reminded people of the vital relationship between creature and creator. The sin and guilt sacrifices enabled the Jews to display their human sense of separation from their holy God.

The prophets pleaded for an extra sacrifice - for practical actions as well as symbolic gestures, for personal morality and legal ritual

As time went by, people began abusing the sacrificial system laid down by Moses. The prophets started to plead for an extra type of sacrifice – for practical actions as well as symbolic gestures, for personal morality *and* legal ritual.

Psalm 50:8-23; 51:16-19; Proverbs 15:8; 21:27; Isaiah 58:1-14; 66:1-4, 18-21; Jeremiah 6:20; 7:21-28; Daniel 3:38-43; Hosea 8:11-13; Amos 5:21-24; & Micah 6:6-8 illustrate this maturing in Israel's knowledge of God.

But Isaiah 1:11-20 expresses it most clearly of all. 'What to me is the multitude of your sacrifices? says the Lord: I have had enough of burnt offerings...I do not delight in the blood of bulls... Bring no more vain offerings...Cease to do evil. Learn to do good. Seek justice. Correct oppression. Defend the fatherless. Plead for the widow.'

Gradually, the Jews came to understand sacrifice as both a ceremony to deal with personal sin and also a continuous holy way of life. This idea reaches its Old Testament climax in the four servant songs of Isaiah (42:1-9; 49:1-6; 50:4-11; & 52:13-53:12).

These prophetic songs present a person whose sacrificial

death deals with the sin of others, and whose sacrificial life is characterized by love, justice, humility and suffering. These extraordinary songs point to Jesus. In fact the whole system of Jewish ritual sacrifices points to him. For they express a need which only he fully satisfies, embody a faith that he alone can justify and – most important of all for this book – demand a lifestyle which only he makes possible.

In the ritual sacrifices, the victim was always a substitute. But the worshippers always had to deny themselves for God. Christ may have died in our place permanently to cover our sin, but self-denial is still the 'ritual' demanded by God of the lives that he rules.

It's a mistake to think that the old sacrificial system has no relevance for our lives today – except in revealing the meaning of Christ's death. The Jews gave their best to God in thanksgiving, dedication, intercession, praise and worship – as well as in repentance and pleas for forgiveness.

And the prophets showed that sacrifice should mean more than a regular offering given out of habit. It should be a way-of-life which affects every thought and action.

These sacrificial principles still stand: the cross has not ended their relevance. We give only from our own property. We give only the best And we give whenever we

> Sacrifice means more than a regular offering given out of religious habit. Sacrifice is a way-of-life which affects every thought and action

approach God. If we want to become givers who please God, we would do well to implement these principles.

TITHES

Tithes were gifts given to provide income partly for the poor and mainly for religious leaders. In Israel, the people gave their sacrifices to God: tithes were additional to sacrifices and went principally to the Levites. The Old Testament doesn't make clear the precise arrangements for the tithes, and the practice seems to have changed through the centuries. However, as with sacrifices, we're concerned here with general principles rather than fine details. We want to learn about God's broad pattern of giving from the way that the Israelites seem to have tithed.

What was tithed

Leviticus 27:30-32 makes it plain that all crops and animals had to be tithed. Whenever the people of Israel harvested their fields or their fruit trees, one tenth of the cereals and fruit had to be given away.

The tithe was one tenth of each Jewish family's annual income

It was the same with their animals. Once a year, the owner counted the animals as they walked to pasture. Every tenth one was given away – this was to ensure that a fair selection was made. The owner couldn't use the tithe to get rid of all the inferior animals. Equally, he didn't have to choose only the best ones.

Crops and young animals were the people's income. They worked all year, and harvested the result. If the harvest was large, so was the tithe. If the crops failed, the tithe was smaller. In practice, the tithe was one tenth of each Jewish family's annual income. If anybody preferred to keep their own crops and pay the tithe in cash, they could; but they had to add 20% to the tithe's value. They weren't permitted to do this with their animal harvest. Flocks and herds had to be tithed in kind.

Tithes are *extra* to sacrifices. The value of an Israelite's sacrifices during the year was not deducted from their tithe

It's vital we grasp the principle that tithes are extra to sacrifices. The value of what a Jewish family had offered in sacrifice during the year was not deducted from their tithe! Instead they sacrificed from the nine-tenths of their income which was left-over after they had given their tithe.

Who received the tithe

The Bible always speaks of the tithe as belonging to God and being given to God. Leviticus 27:30 states, 'All the tithe of the land…is the Lord's: it is holy to the Lord'. In Malachi 3:6-12, God explains that the people are 'robbing God' by not bringing the full tithe.

However, unlike sacrifices, tithes were God's special provision for particular groups of people. Families paid their tithe once a year. For two years in three, they gave it to the Levites and Priests in Jerusalem.

For two years in three, the tithe was given to the Levites and Priests. But in the third year, it was given to the poor

In the third year, they gave it to the poor in their own immediate locality.

Numbers 18:21-32 explains why the Jews' tithes were given to the Levites. 'To the Levites I have given every tithe in Israel for an inheritance, in return for their service in the tent of meeting.'

These officials – because of the nature of their religious status and duties – had no means of income, livelihood, or inheritance. The Levites were full-time auxiliary workers who supported the Priests, cared for the fabric in the Tabernacle and Temple, and organized the feasts and festivals throughout the land.

The Priests, who were far fewer in number, also had no income. They were also provided for by the people's tithe, and they received a tenth of the Levites' share. Numbers

18:25-29 shows that, when they'd received the tithe, the Levites had to give the best tenth to the priests.

The Levites and Priests were the church leaders of their day. And the people's tithe – for two years out of three – was given to enable them to perform their God-given responsibilities. The Levites collected the tithe and gave the best tenth to the priests. Both groups of leaders then stewarded what they'd received so that it would last through the third year when they didn't receive any tithe.

> The people's tithe – for two years out of three – was given to enable the religious leaders to perform their God-given responsibilities

In that third year, instead of being taken to Jerusalem, the tithe was stored in the local towns. Deuteronomy 14:29 shows that it was kept there so that 'the sojourner, the fatherless and the widow, who are within your towns, shall come and eat and be filled; that the Lord your God may bless you in all the work of your hands that you do'.

Why ti ● s were given

People must have given their tithes for a mixture of reasons. Doubtless some tithed eagerly because they recognized that everything belonged to God and they were returning to him what was only his by right. Surely some tithed unwillingly, and did so only because Moses' law said that they must. They'd have preferred to keep their tithe, but they wouldn't disobey the God of Israel.

Some would have tithed joyfully because they wanted to provide for their religious leaders and for the poor. Others would have tithed only out of habit or peer-group pressure.

Yet whatever their different reasons for giving, God promised to bless *all* who tithed *fully* and to curse those who didn't tithe or who tithed less than the full amount. In

Deuteronomy 14:29, Moses urges tithing 'that the Lord your God may bless you in all the work of your hands'.

Despite this holy promise, many people abused God's system of tithing. Malachi 3:2-12 records God's word when the Levites weren't making right offerings and the people were oppressing the poor and thrusting aside foreigners.

'Return to me and I will return to you, says the Lord of hosts. You say, "How shall we return?" Will man rob God? Yet you are robbing me. But you say, "How are we robbing you?" In your tithes and offerings. You are cursed with a curse, for you are robbing me; the whole nation of you. Bring the full tithe into the storehouse, that there may be food in my house. And thereby put me to the test, says the Lord, see if I will not open the windows of heaven for you and pour down for you an overflowing blessing'.

> **God blessed those who tithed fully and cursed those who didn't**

Tithing principles

It's obviously not appropriate for the Church today to try to implement all the details of Moses' law. But the principles behind the law are still highly relevant because they reveal so much of God's heart. For example: we're not meant to make ritual blood sacrifices any more, but we are still called to give our best to God at every opportunity.

So it is with tithing. We shouldn't copy all the details of the Jewish system, but we're foolish to ignore the following four divine principles.

[1] Tithing is only one part of our giving.
[2] Tithing is God's pattern for providing for our church leaders *and* for the poor in our community.
[3] A tithe is ten per cent of our annual income.
[4] God materially blesses those who tithe fully.

There's been tremendous controversy in recent years about tithing. But virtually all the disputes have been about modern details which ignore these four biblical principles.

Tithing is meant to provide an income for modern day priests and levites – and the poor around us. Tithes are not meant to finance buildings or special projects

I believe that God expects all his children today to tithe. But I think that he also wants us to sacrifice and to make freewill offerings on top of giving our tithe.

I believe that tithing is meant specifically to provide income for our modern day priests and levites – and for the poor around us. I think that God wants us to use about two-thirds of our tithe to enable some church leaders to function in priestly ministry (pastoring and teaching) and others to work in levitical ministry (administration and caretaking). And I believe God wants us to make sure that the other third of our tithe is used to provide for the poor in our community.

In the Bible, tithes do *not* go towards buildings or special projects. As we'll see, they're financed out of offerings, and I believe that we should still follow this principle today. God's system of tithing is meant to provide income for people – mostly for those in ministry and some for those who are poor. Just imagine, if we followed this principle today, we'd be able to release about one tenth of all believing families into some type of full-time ministry!

It doesn't matter much how these principles are implemented – the details may vary slightly from place to place. In Israel, the people's tithes for the poor were all collected together. So it seems to make sense for our full tithes to go to our local church and for the leaders to use some of that to provide for the poor. But modern leaders shouldn't forget God's warnings to the Levites in Malachi

3:3 for misusing the tithe!

Whatever we do, we should never forget the principle that God materially blesses those who tithe fully. This shouldn't mean limiting our giving to one tenth of our income.

Tithing fully means giving ten per cent of our income to provide income for leaders – then starting to give sacrificially of our best to God, and making our offerings for special needs and projects. This is the sort

> If we followed the tithing principles today, we'd be able to release about one tenth of all believing families into some type of full-time ministry!

of tithing which God blesses! We see little evidence of divine blessing today only because so few people follow his tithing principles.

FREEWILL OFFERINGS

Freewill offerings formed the third aspect of Israel's giving, and these were usually given for special projects – especially buildings. All gifts – whether sacrifices, tithes or freewill offerings – were understood as being given to God. But while sacrifices were offered directly to God, tithes were given to the religious leaders and the poor, and freewill offerings were made for special projects.

The tabernacle offering

God gave Moses clear instructions for collecting the materials needed to build the Tabernacle. In Exodus 25: 1-4 he says, 'Speak to the people of Israel that they take for me an offering; from every man whose heart makes him willing you shall receive the offering for me. This is the offering you shall receive from them: gold, silver and bronze...'

This was not a tithe: people did not have to give an equal percentage of their income. It was 'freewill': they didn't have to contribute. Those with willing hearts were asked to give as much or as little as they chose.

Exodus 35:1-29 & 36:2-7 describe what happened when Moses obeyed God. Read this passage through carefully, and catch the spirit of a genuine Biblical freewill offering.

> People didn't have to contribute if they didn't want to. Only those with willing hearts were asked to give

The offering was voluntary – the people didn't have to contribute. 'Take from among you an offering to the Lord; whoever is of a generous heart, let him bring the Lord's offering (35:5).'

The offering was specific – everyone knew exactly what was needed. 'Goats' hair, tanned rams' skins, acacia wood, oil for the light, spices for the anointing oil, and onyx stones for the ephod (35-9).'

The offering was purposeful – the Jews knew precisely how their gifts would be used. 'The tabernacle, its tent and covering, its hooks and frames, its bars, pillars and bases; the ark with its poles, the mercy seat... (35:11-19).'

The givers were divinely motivated – only the people moved by God gave. 'They came, every one whose heart stirred him, and every one whose spirit moved him, and brought the Lord's offering to be used for the tent of meeting. So they came, both men and women... (35:21-22).'

> They came – every one whose heart stirred him, and every one whose spirit moved him – and brought the Lord's offering to be used for the tent of meeting

The offering ended when enough had been given. The leaders didn't try to collect more than was needed for the publicly declared purpose of the offering. 'Moses gave command, and word was proclaimed throughout the camp, "Let neither man nor

woman do anything more for the offering for the sanctuary."
So the people were restrained from bringing; for the stuff
they had was sufficient to do all the work (36:3-7).'

The first temple offering

The story of the freewill offering for Israel's first temple is
recorded in 1 Chronicles 28 & 29. Read these chapters and
see how the principles we've noted were followed again.

The people didn't have to contribute – the money wasn't
raised from tithes. 'Who then will offer willingly? (29:5).'

They knew what was needed and how their gifts would be
used. 28:11-19 outlines David's detailed plan of the work
and materials required for the temple. 'All this he made
clear by the writing from the hand of the Lord concerning
it, all the work to be done according to the plan (28:19).'

And all the giving was divinely motivated. 'The people
rejoiced because these had been given willingly, for with a
whole heart they had offered freely to the Lord (29:9).'

The second temple offering

The story of the freewill offerings used to build Israel's
second temple is scattered through Ezra and Nehemiah.

It begins with Cyrus' decree in Ezra 1:2-4. '...let each
survivor, in whatever place he sojourns, be assisted by the
men of his place with silver and gold, with goods and with
beasts, besides freewill offerings for the house of God which
is in Jerusalem.'

The account continues through Ezra 1:5-6; 2:68-69; 3:5;
7:16; & Nehemiah 7:70-72, and shows again how freewill
offerings were God's pattern of giving for providing the
resources for special building projects in Israel.

Freewill offerings for the poor

Although there were occasional gigantic freewill offerings for holy buildings, the Jews were also under a general duty to provide generously for the poor.

Jews were often reminded by God to love strangers, not to oppress them. God gave them two reasons for this: firstly, God loved strangers; and secondly, they knew what it was like to be strangers from their experiences in Egypt.

Deuteronomy 10: 17-19 states 'The Lord your God...is not partial and takes no bribe. He executes justice for the fatherless and the widow, and loves the sojourner, giving him food and clothing. Love the sojourner therefore; for you were sojourners in Egypt.'

The Jews were also instructed to give freely to the poor. Deuteronomy 15:7-11 says that, 'you shall not harden your heart or shut your hand against your poor brother, but you shall open your hand to him...You shall give to him freely, and your heart shall not be grudging when you give to him; because for this the Lord your God will bless you in all your work and in all that you undertake.'

> God executes justice for the fatherless and the widow, and loves the sojourner, giving him food and clothing. Love the sojourner therefore

The same sort of generosity towards strangers and the poor and is spelt out in Deuteronomy 24:10-22. Once again there is a promise of blessing from God for those who give freely to the poor. 'When you reap your harvest in your field, and have forgotten a sheaf in the field, you shall not go back to get it. It shall be for the sojourner, the fatherless and the widow; that the Lord your God may bless you in all the work of your hands.'

It's important for us to recognize that God's promise of blessing here is for those who give generously to provide for those who are poor. Read Isaiah 58:6-11 and see the incredible blessings for those who share their bread with the hungry and bring the homeless poor into their homes.

'If you pour yourself out for the hungry and satisfy the desire of the afflicted *then* shall your light rise in the darkness and your gloom be as the noonday. And the Lord will

> Give to the poor freely, and with a heart which is not grudging. For this the Lord will bless you

guide you continually, and satisfy your desire with good things, and make your bones strong... (58:10-11).'

God doesn't promise to bless those who give to building projects – the building is their blessing, for they can always see it and enjoy it and be blessed when they worship God within it. But he does guarantee to bless those who give generously to the poor and to bless those who follow his tithing principles. Remember, if we want to receive God's blessing, we have to give in God's way.

ISRAEL'S GIVING PRINCIPLES

So we've seen that giving in Israel involved sacrifices, tithes and free-will offerings. Each was for a different and definite purpose, all had distinctive principles, and every Jew was asked to give in *all* three ways.

I've distilled the following five general giving principles from all the detail we've examined.

Summary of principles

1) We should give the best that we have to God every time we approach him.

2) We should give a tenth of our income. The largest chunk to provide income for Christians in full-time

service, and the smaller part to provide resources for the poor nearby.

3) We should give to capital projects only when we are moved by God – and when we know exactly what is needed, why it is needed and what it will be used for.

4) We should give in small practical ways to the poor whenever possible.

5) We should expect our work to be greatly blessed by God.

When we add these Old Testament principles to our understanding of God as the all-giving, all-generous Creator and Redeemer, we'll be well on the way to becoming givers after God's own heart – to becoming blessed and cheerful givers.

GIVERS IN ISRAEL

Giving began with God. In Genesis 3:16-21, God offered Adam and Eve replacement clothes. Animals died to provide the garments. And surely it must have been God who slew, then skinned, some of those perfect creatures which only a short while before he'd created, blessed and described as good.

This incident teaches much about the best Old Testament giving – especially sacrifice. The gift was permanent. The cost to the giver was considerable. Those who benefited were completely undeserving. The giver's loss was absolute. His gift was perfect. His only motives were grace, love and mercy. And those to whom the gift was offered had the freedom to accept or reject the present.

Cain & Abel

The first mention of a human gift is found in Genesis 4:3-5. Both Cain and Abel offered gifts to God, but God looked favorably only on Abel's gift. Cain's was rejected.

Hebrews 11:4 comments, 'By faith Abel offered to God a more acceptable sacrifice than Cain, through which he received approval as righteous, God bearing witness by accepting his gifts'.

What was the difference between the gifts? Why did God accept one and reject the other? Abel gave 'the first-born of his flock and some of their fat as well'. But Cain gave only 'some of the produce of the soil'. Abel seems to have given the best that he had – which always takes faith. While Cain appears to have offered a much less-costly gift.

Abel gave with faith – and then made the astonishing discovery that God gives something back to those who give their best

Neither gift was made to earn God's favor – both were natural attempts to express thanks. But Cain did not risk giving God his best – and was rejected. Whereas Abel gave with faith – and made the astonishing discovery that God gives something back to those who give their best.

Immediately we begin looking at givers in Israel, we learn three new things about giving *to God*. [1] Our gift should be so valuable or important to us personally that we need *faith* to give it. [2] Our gift may be rejected by God if it is less than our best. And [3] God gives something back to those who've given their best in faith to him.

Please note, God's gift of righteous approval to Abel didn't prevent Cain from killing him! In fact, this very gift triggered the jealous anger which made Cain a murderer.

Noah

Noah offered the next recorded gift to God. In Genesis 8:20 we read that, after the Flood had subsided, Noah built the first altar and offered God a great sacrifice. Noah gave the best that he had. He sacrificed 'of every clean animal and every clean bird'. These were creatures that he'd lovingly cared for throughout the flood – one's that he'd planned to use to repopulate the earth. And he gave them up to God – with faith – *in thanks* for his family's safe deliverance.

It was a spontaneous gesture of gratitude by Noah. God

hadn't requested thanks, and he didn't need what was given. However, God was so pleased with Noah's gift that he rewarded him with the promise of fabulous future blessing.

Read these promises in Genesis 8:21-9:17. Pay special attention to verse three where God promises Noah, 'I give you everything'.

God promises, 'I give you everything'

Underline verse seven where God blesses him with these words, 'And you, be fruitful and multiply, bring forth abundantly on the earth and multiply in it'.

These important verses show us that those who give their best to God are unexpectedly repaid in blessing.

Today, sadly, we often think that a spoken 'Thank You' prayer is all that is appropriate when God has helped us in a special way. I promise that we would receive far more of God's blessings if we learnt from men like Noah to express our gratitude in sacrificial giving as well as in words.

Abraham

Abraham teaches us much about giving. For example, he willingly gave Lot first choice of the land (Genesis 13:5-18); he gave a tithe of everything to Melchizedek (14:17-24); and he gave hospitality to strangers (18:1-15). But it is Abraham's giving of his long-promised son Isaac, in Genesis 22, which teaches us the most.

God asked a man for a gift, and he wanted the best

For the first time, God asked a man for a gift. And he wanted the best. Abraham was asked to offer Isaac as a burnt-offering on Mount Moriah – the place where the Jerusalem Temple would eventually be sited.

Isaac, who by then was aged about thirty, was prepared to be the willing victim – to give himself. His elderly father was ready to give his only son. But how pointless the proposed death must have seemed to them both, especially after all God's promises down the years.

By faith Abraham seized the knife and prepared to plunge it into his son. Human reasoning usually concludes that sacrificial giving is stupid. But Abraham believed that God knew best. He didn't understand why God wanted him to give his son. He didn't know that nearly 2,000 years later God would go through similar agonies on exactly the same mountain. Abraham simply acted in faith and prepared to obey his God – and to give him his best.

In verse five, Abraham told his servants that Isaac and he were going to worship. This may seem a very strange word for what Abraham intended to do. But only to those people who don't realize that giving is the essence of worship.

The Hebrew word for worship, *shachah*, means to bow the self down. Many today mistakenly understand worship to mean singing songs, saying prayers and listening to sermons.

But, in Israel, worship meant giving. God is worshipped when our self is bowed before God in recognition that his will is best and accepted with thanksgiving. His will may mean waiting, suffering, even dying, and when these are willingly embraced as part of his mysterious purpose, God is always worshipped.

> Many today mistakenly understand worship to mean singing songs, saying prayers, listening to sermons. But in Israel, worship meant giving

Abraham put aside his plans for Isaac, his reputation with his servants, even his love for his wife. He bowed his self to God's will and prepared to give that which was most precious to him. When he raised the knife he reached heights of worship unknown to most today who regularly raise their arms in praise and prayer.

See how God responded to Abraham's faith-filled willingness to give his only son! Read Genesis 22:15-18 and grasp the link between faith-filled giving and extravagant blessing. Abraham and his son had been ready for death without any hint of reward. They just wanted to please God, and they knew he was pleased by obedient giving. Faithful, selfless, loving obedience was their sole motivation. But, once again, God's grace rewarded man's sacrificial giving with a glorious promise of blessing.

> **God's grace rewarded man's sacrificial giving with a glorious promise of blessing**

This link between blessing and giving sacrificially to God is repeated in Genesis 46:1-4. Jacob's sacrifice at Beersheba was followed by the twin promises of God's presence and considerable future reward.

Ruth

The book of Ruth tells a story which is one of the best biblical examples of the way that God wants us to care for the poor and for foreigners.

We know that, time and again, the people in Israel failed to keep God's law and fell far short of his perfect standards. But in this small book we see one man, Boaz, living the Deuteronomy 24:10-22 rule and being blessed for it in a quite unexpected way.

Ruth – a poor widow from the country of Moab – went into the Bethlehem fields at harvest to collect any barley which had been missed by the harvesters. Not only did Boaz obey the law and allow Ruth to 'glean', he also gave her far more than the law demanded. He provided her with food and refreshment, and told his workers to make sure that they dropped extra barley for her to collect.

The story ends with Boaz marrying the foreigner and the startling revelation that David was their great-grandson. This means that Jesus himself was descended from this act of loving generosity to a poor foreigner. Truly the book of Ruth shows how God blesses those who give to the poor!

Job

We've seen that God announced his blessing at moments in the lives of Old Testament characters when they were giving to him or to the poor. However, it would be wrong to think that God only blessed people when they gave in these ways.

Our gracious God blesses the sinful and the undeserving. Yet some people still think like Job's friends and assume that success and wealth are always the fruit of obedience, and that failure and poverty are always the result of sin. The book of Job shoots down this false idea.

> Some people still think that success and wealth are the fruit of obedience, and that failure and poverty are the result of sin. Job shoots down this false idea

Job was a wealthy man who was 'blameless and upright, one who feared God and turned away from evil' (Job 1:1). There's no embarrassment about his wealth, but it's not presented as a result of his virtue. In fact, Satan suggests in Job 1:6-12 that it's the other way round – that Job served God only because of his wealth.

So God allowed Satan to impoverish Job. He lost his wealth, his health and his family. Yet he didn't turn away from God. Job refused to curse God and reject him. The people around Job insisted that his misfortune must be the result of sin. But it simply wasn't true.

The book ends with Job's fortune being restored twofold (42:10-17). Surely this book is proof that wealth and poverty are not *necessarily* the results of obedience or sin.

Reuel, Manoah & the old man of Gibeah

The Old Testament takes for granted the responsibility of providing and caring for travelers and visitors. We've already noted Abraham's hospitality. In Genesis 18 he treated strangers as honored guests and made the best possible provision for them.

In Exodus 2:16-22, Reuel was surprised that his daughters could meet a stranger and not invite him to a meal. He ordered them to 'call him that he may eat bread'.

He received unknown strangers as honored guests and made the best possible provision for them

Judges 13:15 records how Manoah treated his unknown guest in the same generous way as Abraham. Whereas the Ammonites and Moabites are condemned in Deuteronomy 23:3-6 for failing to treat the traveling Israelites hospitably.

We don't know the name of the old man of Gibeah in Judges 19. Yet he stands out as one of the great biblical examples of giving to visitors.

Not only did he receive a stranger into his home, he also refused to accept any contribution by his guest. And then – when the visitor was threatened by his neighbors – he tried to protect him. It's rather like the story of Lot in Sodom, when his duty as host was greater than his duty as father.

As well as this general responsibility of giving hospitality to strangers and visitors, the people of Israel also had a special duty of providing for God's servants the prophets. We'll see this soon in the lives of men like Elijah and Elisha.

The people of Israel had a special duty to provide for God's servants

David

The Bible never hides the sins or character defects of God's children. If it did, we would despair of ever being useful to him. Instead, the Bible constantly reveals how people sin, fall and rise again to serve God. Nobody in the Old Testament shows this more clearly than David.

David also teaches us a few truths about giving. In 1 Samuel 25 he asks Nabal to provide for his men. Nabal refuses. In anger, David sets out to kill Nabal, only to be stopped by Abigail's generosity. David then sees his error and is glad that he'd been prevented from taking vengeance and killing without cause.

> It's easy to feel angry like David when our pleas for people to give are rejected

It's easy to feel angry like David when our pleas for people to give are rejected and it looks like our plans will fail. We must recognize that sometimes God uses people like Abigail to provide in an unexpected way.

David's burning ambition was to build a house for God in Jerusalem. He longed to do this more than anything else. Yet God made it clear to him, through Nathan the prophet, that it was not God's will for him to build the Temple.

Even though his hopes were dashed, David didn't sulk or get angry. Instead he made thorough preparations and gave as generously as he could – so that another could have the fame and glory of building God a house. 1 Chronicles 22:2-16 & 29:2-5 catalogue the extent of David's astonishing giving which enabled Solomon to build his dream project.

There's a vital lesson here for us today. We should learn to give with David's generosity so that others are enabled to accomplish what we had hoped to achieve ourselves.

Solomon

David's son built the Temple. It took Solomon twenty years to complete, and during that time he became a byword for wealth. The Bible devotes much space to listing Solomon's riches and concludes that he 'excelled all the kings of the earth in riches and wisdom' (1 Kings 10:23).

The Queen of Sheba's famous visit highlights Solomon's affluence. In 1 Kings 10:7 she says, 'I did not believe the reports until I came and my own eyes had seen it; and, behold, the half was not told me. Your wisdom and prosperity surpass the report which I heard.'

There's no mystery about Solomon's wealth. 1 Kings 3:13 makes it clear that it was a gift from God. 'I give you also what you have not asked, both riches and honor, so that no other king shall compare with you, all your days.'

Sadly, the Bible doesn't record one instance of Solomon giving anything to anybody. His harsh policies ensured that he lost the good-will and loyalty of the Israelites. And his foreign wives led him to break his covenant with God.

Despite all his God-given wisdom and wealth, Solomon stands as an example of a man who never learnt to give.

Despite all his God-given wisdom and wealth, Solomon stands as an example of a man who never learnt to give

Elijah and Elisha

A succession of incidents in these two men's lives show the importance of providing for God's servants the prophets.

After Elijah had announced the drought, in 1 Kings 17:1, he was sent to the brook Cherith where God provided for him. Next, God sent Elijah to Zarapheth, in the neighboring country of Sidon, where he met a very poor widow. Elijah asked her for food and drink, but she was at the end of her natural resources and expecting to die soon from hunger.

Elijah told the widow to make a cake with the last of her flour and oil, and to give it to him. Afterwards she could prepare food for her family. He promised that God would bless her by miraculously supplying her needs when she gave her all to God's servant.

The woman did as requested – and provided us with a wonderful example of faith-filled sacrificial giving.

This is very important story for us today, because it clearly shows how God blesses those people who give faithfully and sacrificially to God's servants.

The widow was not a wealthy person. She had virtually nothing and no prospects of anything except death from starvation. The prophet did not ask her for much in the world's eyes, only 'a morsel of bread'. Yet this was more than the woman could humanly afford. The prophet urged her to give by promising her that her 'jar of meal shall not be spent, and the cruse of oil shall not fail, until the day that the Lord sends rain upon the earth' (1 Kings 17:14).

Elijah promised that God would miraculously supply the widow's needs when she gave her all to God's servant

This would have seemed a ridiculous promise to anybody listening. They would have thought that Elijah was tricking her into giving him her last piece of food. But Elijah was a prophet. He spoke at God's prompting. What he promised came true. When the woman acted in faith on his words, she discovered that his God was completely reliable. In fact she was better off after giving than if she hadn't given!

In the next chapter, 1 Kings 18, we learn about Obadiah who – at enormous risk to himself – provided generously for one hundred of God's prophets!

The Bible records several similar incidents in Elisha's life. 2 Kings 4 is one of the most critical chapters about giving in the Old Testament. It records three stories which each teach us something vital about finances for today.

Verses 1-8 show how God miraculously helps people to

be released from debt. A widow turned to Elisha for advice and help. He had no money himself to pay her debts, but instead he gave her God's plan of action. It would have seemed foolish to her neighbors, but it was God's provision for her need.

When she acted in faith on the prophet's instructions she was able to do as Elisha had said, 'Go, sell the oil and pay your debts, and you and your sons can live on the rest'.

> When she acted in faith on the prophet's instructions she was able to clear her debts

Verses 8-17 tells the story of a wealthy woman who, first, regularly gave Elisha food, and then built an extension on her home especially for him.

Once more we read how God blessed a woman for her generosity to one of God's servants. It's clear that God's gift to her of a son was a personal reward for her giving. If she hadn't given she would have remained childless. When the son died, his healing was clearly linked to her generosity.

Never let anyone persuade us that giving to God's servants the prophets can't have wonderful consequences!

The third incident in 2 Kings 4 introduces a man from Baalshalishah. Verses 42-44 describe how the man thought that he was providing for one prophet and was amazed when God used his giving to provide for one hundred prophets!

> Never let anyone persuade us that giving to God's servants the prophets can't have wonderful consequences!

When we give to God's servants today we should expect God to use our gifts in a wonderful way which is far beyond our wildest hopes and intentions. In God's miraculous hands, even the smallest gift makes an enormous difference.

Elijah and Elisha teach us two other principles about giving. 1 Kings 21 reports Naboth's sad story. He owned a vineyard which was coveted by King Ahab. The king asked Naboth to sell him the vineyard, and became very 'vexed and sullen' when Naboth refused to do this.

> In God's hands, even the smallest gift makes an enormous difference

Ahab's wife caused Naboth to be killed and the king took possession of the vineyard. So God sent Elijah to announce an awesome judgment on Ahab and his wife. The terrible truth is that God curses those who take, as well as blessing those who give.

2 Kings 5 tells the well-known story of Naaman's cure. The postscript to the story, in verses 15-27, adds to our understanding of giving. Naaman wanted to reward God's prophet for the miracle. But Elisha refused: 'As the Lord lives, whom I serve, I will receive none' (5:16).

Elisha's assistant, Gehazi, was tempted by the offered gift. He went after Naaman, pretended that Elisha had changed his mind, and accepted an enormous sum of money – which he kept for himself. Gehazi lied when Elisha questioned him about this, and Elisha announced a fearsome judgment on his assistant. Truly God curses those who mislead people to attract giving.

> Naaman's gift was simply too large. Elisha didn't need such a vast sum of money

Many may wonder why it was right for the Shunammitess to give to Elisha but wrong for Naaman. 2 Kings 5:26 supplies the answer. 'Was it a time to accept money and garments, olive orchards and vineyards, sheep and oxen, menservants and maidservants?'

Naaman's gift was simply too large. Elisha didn't need

such a vast sum of money. A principle runs through the Old Testament that giving to people and projects should meet needs and no more. Giving should stop when the need has been met. We saw this in the tabernacle free-will offering, and we've seen that Jewish giving to people always matched their needs. Only sacrificial giving directly to God was allowed to be lavish.

Nehemiah

Nehemiah 5:14-19 shows a different aspect of giving and receiving – but one that is dreadfully relevant today.

Here Nehemiah reports that he didn't take advantage of his position to accept a high salary or excessive expenses. He didn't ask for gifts from the people. He refrained from acquiring land, and didn't even eat the food allowance of the governor. Why? 'Because the servitude was heavy upon this people.'

Too many leaders today take advantage of their positions. They pay themselves high salaries and accept lavish gifts at a time when debt, unemployment and inflation have placed another heavy servitude on most ordinary people. They would do well to learn from Nehemiah and Elisha.

Summary of principles

What can we learn from these Old Testament givers? I've distilled these principles from the detail we've examined.

1) We shouldn't say just 'Thank You' to God. We should lavishly give him our best in thanksgiving too.

2) We should remember to give to God's servants the prophets – but only to meet their needs.

3) We should provide for the poor whenever we can.

4) We should give in a way which means we need faith.

5) We should make hospitality a special priority.

6) We should always remember that giving to God is the essence of worship.

7) We should expect God to bless us – materially and spiritually – when we give in the way that he wants.

8) We should expect God to curse us when we take what's not ours or mislead people to attract a gift.

Let's add these principles to what we've learnt so far – and ensure that we benefit from what we've read about these Old Testament characters. After all, their lives have been recorded in Scripture so that we can profit from their examples.

THE SUPREME GIVER

Jesus spoke about money more often than any subject other than the kingdom of God. Even in his day, the subject of giving was controversial, and Jesus gave an amazing amount of time to dealing with financial questions.

We're even told that he 'sat down opposite the treasury and watched the multitude putting money into the treasury' (Mark 12:41). Jesus deliberately watched what people gave, discerned the spirit in which they gave, and then commented on it.

First we'll examine Jesus' teaching about giving. Then we'll look at his encounters with people when he applied his principles about giving to their different real-life situations.

All I'm going to do in this chapter is point out God's word. Jesus' teaching about giving is incredibly clear and straightforward. I'm not going to insert any qualifications. I'm not going to pretend that it can't apply today. I'm not going to dilute it or explain it away. I'm simply going to show that his teaching is both frightening and exciting.

We'll see that his words are the opposite of modern-day wisdom. They fly in the face of almost everything we've learnt – with awesome implications. But they only make sense when we grasp a fundamental biblical principle: money isn't neutral, it's a *power* with a life of its own.

In Matthew 6:24, Jesus baldly states that we 'cannot serve God and *mammon*'. His use of the Aramaic word *mammon* personifies money as a rival to God and makes it crystal clear that wealth is neither neutral or impersonal. *Mammon* is a power which attempts to dominate and enslave us.

A powerful false-God

This means that there are spiritual forces *behind* the material form of money. These forces have a seductive power which grips people's lives. They're the cause of our difficulties in giving money away. They explain why wealth seems to strip us of compassion and kindness. And they are the basic reason why so much of Jesus' teaching about money is given in an evangelistic setting.

Today, we often think of money as a topic for Christian discipleship rather than as a part of the conversion process. That wasn't so with Jesus. Time and again he insists that a financial change is required if people are to follow him; that wealth is an idol which has to be rejected and replaced with the living God; that riches are the reason why so much spiritual fruit fails to mature.

There are spiritual forces behind money with a power which grips people's lives. They're the reason why we find it hard to give money away

For Jesus, the power of money is a false-God from which people must be converted, and the love of riches is a weed which chokes too many seedlings. The rejection of *mammon* is a basic requirement of being his disciple.

Wealth makes people feel secure. It seems to give freedom, power and contentment. It can even us feel guilty. People everywhere seek it furiously. But God wants us to find our security, freedom, power and contentment in Christ alone – and to seek him with our whole heart.

If we don't grasp this principle we won't understand Jesus'

teaching. He labels honest, prudent, hardworking, wealthy folk as fools. He rejects decent, moral, spiritually interested rich people. It doesn't make sense until we realize that they're individuals who need to be redeemed from their slavery to the false-God *Mammon*. Only then can their wealth be used for the good of God's kingdom.

Jesus' giving teaching

God sent John the Baptist to prepare the way for Jesus. He preached a baptism of repentance for the forgiveness of sins, telling the crowds who came to him to 'bear fruits that befit repentance' (Luke 3:8).

Fruit of repentance

Quite naturally, 'the multitudes asked him, "What then shall we do?" And he answered them, "He who has two coats, let him share with him who has none; and he who has food, let him do likewise."' (Luke 8:10-11). John told tax collectors that their repentance needed to be evidenced by collecting no more than the appointed sums, and he taught soldiers that their repentance should be seen in contentment with their pay.

How many modern-day preachers would give John's answer to the same question? How many teachers insist today that new converts should *give* as their basic response to the gospel?

John makes it plain that repentance should make a difference – a difference which is seen primarily in finances – by both giving away *and* not demanding more than is right.

John's teaching suddenly makes sense when we understand that money is a false-God. And so does Jesus' famous remark in Matthew 19:23-26 that it's 'easier for a camel to go through the eye of a needle than for a rich man to enter the kingdom of God'.

These words can only be true if there is a financial aspect to conversion – if *giving* is the vital evidence of genuine biblical repentance.

Part of commitment

Time and again Jesus asks people to turn from their wealth – from their slavery to *mammon* – to express their commitment to him. Levi willingly left everything (Luke 5:27-28) but the rich young ruler found the demand too much (Luke 18:18-23).

Jesus' principle was that those who wanted to be committed to him had to understand that 'foxes have holes, and birds of the air have nests; but the Son of man has nowhere to lay his head' (Luke 9:58).

The calling of Simon, Andrew, James and John – in Luke 5:1-11 – makes this principle particularly clear. Following Jesus' advice, the four men caught so large a shoal of fish that their nets began to break and their boats started to sink. In fact Simon was so astonished by the miraculous catch that he fell at Jesus' knees in fear.

The catch would have considerably boosted their income. But what did they do? Keep it or give it away? The Bible says that 'they left *everything* and followed him'.

Instead of benefiting personally from God's miraculous provision, they left the fish on the shore for others. This was their way of expressing their commitment to Jesus.

Instead of benefiting from God's miraculous provision, they left the fish on the shore for others. This was an expression of their commitment to Jesus

Part of ministry

Jesus continually urged his disciples to reject *mammon*. Matthew, Mark and Luke all record Jesus' instructions when he sent his disciples on their first ministry tour.

Jesus told them to 'preach as you go, saying, "The kingdom of heaven is at hand". Heal the sick. Raise the dead. Cleanse lepers. Cast out demons. You received without paying, give without pay. Take no gold, nor silver, nor copper in your belts,

> Preach the kingdom, heal the sick, raise the dead, cleanse lepers, cast out demons. You received without paying, give without pay

no bag for your journey, nor two tunics, nor sandals, nor a staff; for the laborer deserves his food (Matthew 10:7-10).'

Should we now pick and choose between these instructions? Many leaders urge believers to preach, heal, and cast out demons, but then are silent about giving without pay. Surely it would be better if they urged people to obey *all* these commands.

The twelve were sent as givers – for every part of ministry is a gift. And just as they'd received without paying from Jesus, so they were to give without charging to others. This follows on from the principles we saw in Elijah and Elisha.

But how were they to survive? Matthew 10:11 gives the answer: hospitality. They weren't to charge, but they could accept gifts which related to their immediate needs.

Jesus gave similar instructions to a much larger group of disciples in Luke 10:1-12. They were ordered not to take a purse or bag to collect gifts; but they were told to accept whatever hospitality was offered to them.

Treasure in heaven

At the end of his instructions to his disciples, in Matthew 10:40-42, Jesus makes it plain that people who provide hospitality for them will be rewarded by God. This repeats what we saw in the Old Testament.

But what are these rewards for giving God's servants hospitality? And when will they be received? Jesus' words are plain and not easily misunderstood.

In the middle of the Sermon on the Mount – that wonderful collection of kingdom principles – Jesus orders this. 'Do not lay up for yourselves treasures on earth, where moth and rust consume and where thieves break in and steal. But lay up for yourselves treasure in heaven, where neither moth nor rust consumes and where thieves do not break in and steal. For where your treasure is, there will your heart be also (Matthew 6: 19-21).'

It's a straightforward choice: earthly or heavenly treasure. Only two verses later Jesus says, 'No one can serve two masters; for either he will hate the one and love the other, or he will be devoted to the one and despise the other. You cannot serve God and *mammon*.'

When Jesus puts it like this we know it makes sense to choose God, to choose heavenly treasure. Yet the spiritual power *mammon* makes it hard for us to resist the temptation to lay up earthly treasures.

In Luke 12:33-34, Jesus explains how we can defeat the devil with one blow. Giving is the spiritual weapon which – at the same time – both earns us heavenly treasure and breaks the power of *mammon*.

> **Giving is the weapon which – at the same time – earns us heavenly treasure and breaks the power of *mammon***

'Sell your possessions and give alms. Provide yourselves with purses that do not grow old, with a treasure in the heavens that does not fail.'

It's impossible for it be plainer that giving is God's way to earn heavenly treasure. But note that it's *heavenly* treasure.

Jesus doesn't promise here that giving will earn us *earthly* treasure. Instead he asks what we want. Heavenly or earthly treasure? If we want earthly

> If we prefer heavenly treasure, we'll give and give, and go on giving like God

treasure, we should lock up our purses, keep a tight hold of our possessions and never give alms. But if we prefer heavenly treasure, we'll give and we'll give, and we'll go on giving like God.

Give to the needy

Jesus' famous parable of the sheep and the goats develops our understanding of blessing and heavenly treasure. In Matthew 25:34, the sheep are welcomed into heaven as the 'blessed of my Father', while in 25:41 the goats are banished into eternal fire as 'you cursed'.

The blessed ones are rewarded with the gift of a kingdom. The cursed are punished with eternal fire. But why are some blessed and others cursed?

Jesus' parable is too clear to misunderstand. The sheep are blessed with a kingdom because the king 'was hungry and you gave me food. I was thirsty and you gave me drink. I was a stranger and you welcomed me. I was naked and you clothed me. I was sick and you visited me. I was in prison and you came to me.'

This reward takes the sheep completely by surprise. They have no recollection of ever giving to the king in this way. There must be some sort of mistake. 'And the king will answer them, "Truly, I say to you, as you did it to one of the least of these my brethren, you did it to me.'

It's the same for the goats. They're cursed because the king was hungry and they did not feed him, he was thirsty and they gave him no drink – and so on.

The cursed are mystified. They're sure that they've never

ignored the king in this way. They would have given to him if they thought that he needed their gifts. The terrible reply rings down the centuries. 'As you did it *not* to one of the least of these, you did it *not* to me.'

Heavenly treasure, the promise of a kingdom, divine blessing, holy rewards – all these depend on how we give to God. And that's measured by our generosity to *people*. Is it little wonder that I stress giving so much? Surely we can all see now that giving is vital for our spiritual health – and absolutely essential for our spiritual wealth.

> **Heavenly treasure, divine blessing, a kingdom, holy rewards – all these depend on our generosity to people. Little wonder that I stress giving so much!**

In Luke 11:42 Jesus makes it clear that tithing isn't enough. 'Woe to you Pharisees! For you tithe mint and rue and every herb, and neglect justice and the love of God. These you ought to have done, without neglecting the others.' Although the Pharisees tithed carefully, they stopped there. That wasn't enough for Jesus. He wanted them to go further, to give more to the needy.

The parable of the Good Samaritan, in Luke 10:29-37, has inspired many people through the ages. But remember, it was told to an expert in Jewish laws who would have tithed faithfully. He was told to give more, to stretch his understanding of neighbors to include despised, non-believing enemies, and to make practical provision for them.

The Samaritan didn't toss the victim a few shekels. He touched the wounded enemy, gave him first aid, took him to an inn, cared for him, gave two days' wages for his keep, and promised to return to pay any outstanding bill. He gave time, love and energy – as well as money. And Jesus tells us to 'go and do likewise'.

Jesus ties some of these principles together in Luke 16. He instructs us to 'make friends for yourselves by means of unrighteous *mammon*, so that when it fails they may receive you into the eternal habitations' (16:9). Jesus explains that 'if you have not

> Generous giving doesn't save us, it shows that we have been saved

been faithful in the unrighteous *mammon*, who will entrust to you the true riches?' (16:11). He repeats his principle that 'you cannot serve God and *mammon*' (16:13). Jesus then illustrates all this with his parable of the rich man and Lazarus (16:19-31).

People like the rich man are hardhearted towards people like Lazarus because – whether they realize it or not – they serve the false-God *mammon*. Such people will not enter heaven.

People who serve the true God have been released by him from their slavery to *mammon* – and they show this by giving with God's generosity and compassion. They will have much treasure in heaven. But remember, generous giving doesn't save us, it shows that we have been saved.

Give to all who ask

Jesus starkest teaching on giving comes in his Sermon on the Mount. 'Give to him who begs from you, and do not refuse him who would borrow from you'. (Matthew 5:42).

Is there another verse in the Bible so opposed to the spirit of our age? I doubt it. How many believers are there in our churches who think that these words of Jesus are a good idea? Nothing shows people's slavery to *mammon* more clearly than their reaction to this statement.

> Nothing shows people's slavery to *mammon* more clearly than their reaction to these words

73

Jesus' words are even stronger in Luke 6:30. 'Give to *every one* who begs from you; and of him who takes away your goods do not ask them again.' Why should we give like this? Why does Jesus not allow us some exceptions. Why should there be no limits to our giving?

Jesus has two answers. We should be able to guess them by now. [1] Because this is precisely how God gives. [2] Because there are fantastic blessings for giving like this.

'Love your enemies, and do good, and lend, expecting nothing in return; and your reward will be great, and you will be sons of the Most High. For he is kind to the ungrateful and the selfish (Luke 6:35).'

Three verses later there's a more popular verse. 'Give, and it will be given to you; good measure, pressed down, shaken together, running over, will be put into your lap.'

> **Give, and it will be given to you; good measure, pressed down, shaken together, running over, will be put into your lap**

This saying should not be lifted out of context. The great rewards Jesus lists in verse 38 relate to the giving he has just described in verse 30. This means that it's not only our giving to friends which attracts this wonderful blessing, it's also our giving to beggars, enemies and ungrateful sinners. We should realize that we can only claim the Luke 6:38 blessing when we give like God and are giving to *everyone* who asks us.

Give privately

In Matthew 6:1-3, Jesus describes *how* we should give. 'Beware of practising your piety before men in order to be seen by them; for then you will have *no* reward from your Father who is in heaven. Thus, when you give alms, sound no trumpet before you, as the hypocrites do in the synagogues and streets, that they may be praised by men.

Truly, I say to you, they have received their reward. But when you give alms, do not let your left hand know what your right hand is doing, so that your alms may be in secret, and your Father who sees in secret will reward you.'

Jesus' principle is simple. We forfeit our heavenly reward whenever we publicize our generosity. The human acclaim that we're bound to receive for our giving is deemed to be enough.

> We forfeit our heavenly reward if we publicize our giving to the needy

This is a vital principle now that so many people want their giving to be acknowledged in a public way. Jesus does not condemn those who broadcast their giving on television, in brochures or on wooden panels. He just says that their fame is their reward – they won't get another blessing from God.

Give hospitality

We've seen that the Old Testament takes for granted the responsibility of providing and caring for visitors. Jesus also seems to assume that hospitality is so basic a human duty that he doesn't need to emphasize it.

When he sent his disciples to minister he presumed that they would be provided with hospitality. And the gospels record many occasions when Jesus accepted meals and rest from different people.

Jesus gave his only teaching on hospitality at one such meal. 'When you give a dinner or banquet, do not invite your friends or your brothers or your kinsmen or your rich neighbors, lest they invite you in return and you be repaid. But when you give a feast, invite the poor, the

> When you give a feast, invite the poor, the maim, the lame, the blind, and you will be blessed, because they cannot repay you

maim, the lame, the blind, and you will be blessed, because they cannot repay you. You will be repaid at the resurrection of the just (Luke 14:12-14).'

It's the same two principles we've seen running through Jesus' teaching about giving. [1] Giving to the needy should be a priority – for in that way we're giving to God. [2] We should give in a way which earns heavenly treasure rather than an earthly reward.

Again Jesus offers us a choice. We can restrict our gift of hospitality to those people who'll probably give us something back in return on earth – and receive no reward from God. Or we can also open our homes to the poor and needy – and have a substantial reward in heaven. Our actions reveal where our treasure is, where our heart is.

Give to governments

Jesus taught the people to give their taxes to the relevant authorities. Matthew 22:15-22, Mark 12:13-17 and Luke 20:20-26 all report Jesus' well-known principle 'Render to Caesar the things that are Caesar's, and to God the things that are God's.' The Jews – like all people in their situation – resented giving their money to the occupying power. But Jesus settled the tax question for all time: we must pay up, but without any hint of a heavenly reward.

Matthew 17:24-27 records God's miraculous provision to Jesus and Peter for their annual half-shekel tax payment. This was levied on all Jews for the upkeep of the Temple. This shows three things – that tithes were not used to maintain the Temple, that Jesus did not shirk his financial responsibilities, and that God provides money miraculously.

Give debt release

Debt is a form of slavery which imprisons millions of people. Jesus shows his understanding of this by placing debt release in the middle of the Lord's Prayer. Would he ask us to pray for this if there was no chance of God answering our prayer. Elisha has already shown us how important this is to God.

Two phrases in the prayer are basic to giving. 'Give us this day our daily bread. And forgive us our debts as we also have forgiven our debtors (Matthew 6:11-12).' God wants us to ask him for

> God wants us to ask him for two things: basic food and debt release. But we must forgive all who are in debt to us

two things vital to our well-being. Basic food and debt release. If we can expect God to provide us with food, we can also expect him to release us from debt. There's only one condition – we must forgive those who are in debt to us.

It should be obvious why we're called to behave like this. It's how God acts. Jesus illustrates this with a parable in Matthew 18:23-35. Although it's a story about general forgiveness, it shows that we should release people from any indebtedness they have to us. We are to forgive their debts because God has forgiven our debt. Verse 35 contains a warning for those who don't offer this gift.

Jesus' giving encounters

The four gospels record many instances when men and women gave to Jesus, when he urged people to give, and when he commented on their giving. We're going to examine these encounters to see what principles they teach us about our giving today.

The wise men

The Christmas carol 'We three kings' has popularized many wrong ideas about the men who visited Jesus in Matthew 2:9-12. The Bible doesn't state how many there were or what their status was. All we know for certain is that an unknown number of wise men or astrologers brought treasure chests from their country in the East.

On arriving, they 'fell down and worshipped him. Then, opening their treasures, they offered him gifts, gold and frankincense and myrrh.'

How did they worship Jesus? By singing a hymn? Praying a prayer? Listening to a sermon? No! They gave him a generous offering! That was their way of worshipping.

Read the passage and notice that they gave their very best and thought hard about what to give.

They had been convinced in advance that the infant was a king, so they'd brought gifts with them worthy of his royal status. They gave gold, then the most valuable substance on earth. Gold had been used in the tabernacle to represent God's heavenly glory and his presence on earth. Its use by the men indicated that they thought the child would bring God's glory to earth.

They picked out sweet frankincense to show that the child was a man whose life would ascend, like a ritual sacrifice, as sweet-smelling incense to God. And they were inspired to give bitter myrrh – universally recognized as a symbol of suffering – to suggest that the child would suffer in life and die a terrible death.

This was no casual giving. This was sacrifice. This was faith-filled worship. Clearly they'd thought long and hard about what they should bring on their journey. Then, on seeing Jesus, they were inspired to select the best and most appropriate gifts. There are few better examples of giving in the Bible for us to follow than these pagan astrologers.

The anointing women

Each of the four gospels reports a story of a woman who worshipped Jesus by anointing him. It's difficult to know whether they are recording the same event or different ones. But it doesn't matter for us in our study of giving because they all illustrate similar principles.

Luke 7:36-50 describes Jesus' encounter with a woman who was a sinner with a very bad reputation in her town. She interrupted a meal to wash Jesus' feet with her tears, dry them with her hair, and anoint them with ointment from an alabaster flask.

It's obvious from the parable Jesus told that this woman's motive for giving was a great love which stemmed from her acceptance of God's forgiveness. Although Luke doesn't use the word 'worship', that's clearly what she was doing.

Yet the people who saw her giving were outraged. They didn't think that Jesus should accept a gift from someone like her. But Jesus commended her faith-filled giving: 'Your faith has saved you; go in peace'.

Matthew and Mark tell a slightly different story, and John adds a few extra details. Matthew 26:6-13, Mark 14:3-9, & John 12:1-11 all describe an anointing at Bethany.

Mary anointed Jesus with an incredibly expensive ointment: 300 denarii was almost a year's wages for a laborer. This act of worship was probably a 'Thank You' for her brother's raising from

> This woman's motive for giving was a great love which stemmed from her acceptance of God's forgiveness

the dead. Yet it caused an outrage. People thought that her extravagant gift was a waste of money and should have been used for the poor. Jesus disagreed. He said, 'Let her alone. Why do you trouble her? She has done a beautiful thing to me. For you always have the poor with you, and wherever you will you can do good to them. But you will not always have me. She has done what she could; she has anointed my body beforehand for burying (Mark 14:6-8).'

> This act of worship caused an outrage. People thought it should have been used for the poor. Jesus disagreed

There'll always be criticism when people worship Jesus with extravagant gifts. There'll always be critics who think that money could have been better spent on the poor. But this passage reminds us of the Old Testament principle that we should give lavish sacrificial gifts to God *and* practical gifts to the poor which are appropriate to their needs.

This woman was inspired to offer a gift which had a prophetic meaning far beyond her dreams. Let her worship inspire us. When we're prompted to give a big gift to God, let's do it. It'll be our beautiful action for Jesus.

The generous women

How did Jesus survive financially? He traveled constantly in Israel after he stopped working as a carpenter – much of the time with the twelve apostles. They needed food to eat and somewhere to sleep. But who gave so that Jesus could train his apostles, teach the crowds and heal the sick?

The gospels are full of instances when people provided Jesus and the twelve with hospitality. It seems likely that Jesus usually stayed with Mary, Martha and Lazarus when he was visiting Jerusalem. We read about them in Luke 10:38-42 and in John 11:1-45 & 12:1-12.

This must have been a very wealthy family to have been able to offer hospitality to such a large group of men so frequently – and for Mary to afford such a generous thank-offering when she anointed Jesus with ointment.

These three are not condemned in any way for their wealth. In fact, they are commended for using it wisely. They do not serve *mammon*. They have conquered *mammon* and now use their money to serve God.

Luke 8:1-3 lists some people who financed Jesus' activities. Mary, Joanna, Susanna 'and many others who provided for them out of their resources'.

Remember, these were Jews who paid their tithes and made their sacrifices. Their giving to Jesus was extra. It was additional to their taxes, tithes, freewill offerings and ritual sacrifices. It's giving which follows the Elijah and Elisha principle and makes special provision for God's servants.

> They are commended for using their wealth wisely. They do not serve *mammon*. They have conquered *mammon* and use it to serve God

A rich man

We've seen that Jesus told his disciples it was hard for a rich man to enter the kingdom. He didn't say it was impossible. Matthew 27:57-60 introduces us to 'a rich man from Arimathea, named Joseph, who also was a disciple of Jesus'.

Mark 15:42-47 and Luke 23:50-54 describe his visit to Pilate, his courageous request for Jesus' body, and his gift to Jesus of his very own tomb. John 19:38-40 shows that he was helped by Nicodemus – who gave a hundred pounds of myrrh and aloes – to bury Jesus.

This may seem a strange gift. But we saw earlier that God's giving is creative and varied – and this is an example of the human equivalent. Our giving shouldn't be stereotyped. It should be specific, God-directed and for a clear purpose. Here we have two rich men giving exactly what was needed because they were devoted to Jesus.

Jesus received gifts from pagan astrologers, dreadful sinners, wealthy families, committed followers and secret admirers

The gospels suggest that Nicodemus and Joseph were 'secret' disciples. But that didn't invalidate their giving. We've seen that Jesus received gifts from a mixture of givers – pagan astrologers, dreadful sinners, wealthy families, committed followers, and now from secret admirers. They all have two things in common. They gave their best because of their love. And they took considerable risks in their giving – which means that they gave in faith.

A confused pair

Luke 24:13-35 tells the story of Cleopas and his companion, who gave hospitality to Jesus without realizing who he was.

It's a perfect example of the principle which Jesus outlines in Matthew 10:40, 25:31-46 & Mark 9:41. They willingly gave hospitality to a stranger and discovered that they'd actually offered it to the king!

They gave hospitality to a stranger and discovered they'd offered it to the king!

The pair were confused and disappointed. Their hopes had been dashed by Jesus' crucifixion, and now they couldn't understand what had happened to the body. They chatted with a stranger on their journey and offered him a bed for the night. They didn't think that they were doing anything unusual. They simply opened their home to a stranger and offered him food.

That's all hospitality is. And – as Cleopas discovered – when we entertain strangers we're really giving to our king.

A rich aristocrat

Jesus' encounter with this rich young man is one of the saddest stories in the Bible. Matthew 19:16-22, Mark 10:17-22 & Luke 18:18-23 describe what happened.

A ruler asked Jesus, 'What shall I do to inherit eternal life?' It's a question which is still put to thousands of teachers today. But how many give the same answer as Jesus?

Jesus told the ruler to keep the commandments – and the man replied that he'd observed them all from his youth.

'Jesus, looking upon him, loved him, and said to him, "You lack one thing; go, sell what you have, and give to the poor, and you will have treasure in heaven; and come, follow me (Mark 10:21-22).'

The man was good. The man wanted to follow Jesus. The man was loved by Jesus. But Jesus couldn't let him come without rejecting the false-God *mammon*.

The man had to choose. It was God or his possessions. And when Jesus put it like that he preferred his possessions

'At that saying his countenance fell, and he went away sorrowful; for he had great possessions.' The man tithed. He made his sacrifices. He probably gave to the poor. But that wasn't enough for Jesus. The man had to choose. It was God or his possessions. It was earth or heaven. And when Jesus put it like that the man found that he preferred his earthly possessions to the thought of treasure in heaven.

Jesus didn't chase after the man. He didn't say that a tithe would be enough. He let him walk away because the man wouldn't reject *mammon*, wouldn't become a faith-filled cheerful giver.

Now I know that Jesus didn't say this to everybody he

met. We don't all have to give everything away before we can follow Jesus. But some people do.

This rich man shows us that Jesus is deadly serious about giving. It's not a small matter to him. It's fundamental to his kingdom. If we can't give generously; if we won't give generously, if we *don't* give generously, we need to ask ourselves whether we're closer to *mammon* than God.

A joyful man

Luke takes us straight from this rich man to Zacchaeus. It's a deliberate contrast. First we meet a wealthy ruler who won't give and walks sadly away. Then in Luke 19:1-10 we meet another wealthy man, but this time one who will give. The pages of the gospel almost explode with joy!

Zacchaeus was 'a chief tax collector and rich' who 'sought to see who Jesus was'. But he was unpopular in Jericho. Jesus saw him up a tree and said, '"Zacchaeus, make haste and come down; for I must stay at your house today." So he made haste and came down, and received him joyfully.'

Again crowds complained because Jesus was receiving from a sinner. But Zacchaeus gave a wonderful response. 'Lord, the half of my goods I give to the poor; and if I have defrauded any one of anything, I restore it fourfold.' Jesus hadn't asked the tax collector to give his goods away. He hadn't made giving a condition. Instead, extravagant generosity was Zacchaeus' natural response to Jesus. Faith-filled giving was the fruit of his turning to Christ.

> Overflowing generosity was Zacchaeus' natural response to Jesus. Giving was the fruit of his turning to Christ

Jesus' delight jumps out of the pages of the gospel. 'Today salvation has come to this house, since he also is a son of Abraham. For the Son of man came to seek and to save the lost.'

In this wonderful story we see a rich man breaking free from the grip of *mammon*. He gives to Jesus. He gives to the poor. He gives to all he has defrauded. Most people today would be terrified to do what Zacchaeus did. And imagine the rumpus if I asked people to act like this! Yet what was the outcome? Joy and salvation! Zacchaeus is a wonderful example of a blessed and very cheerful giver.

The betrayer

The story of Judas should be enough to convince remaining skeptics of *mammon's* power. Who betrayed Jesus? What prompted him to betray? Why did he betray him? The treasurer. Greed. Money. It was *mammon* at work.

John 12:4-6 explains that Judas Iscariot had been given responsibility of the common fund by Jesus. Judas had been called by Jesus. He was one of those

Judas took from the money box and did not care for the poor. The betrayer was a taker, not a giver

who'd left everything to follow him. He'd seen Jesus work miracles. God had even worked miracles through Judas on the ministry tour. He'd heard Jesus' teaching. He'd been blessed and used by God. But the struggle between the true God and the false-God *mammon* ended with Judas betraying Jesus for money.

John 12:6 is a terrible epitaph for any disciple with its comments that Judas did not care for the poor and took from the money box. The betrayer was a taker, not a giver.

The sum offered by the priests was five months' wages for a laborer – in modern terms around £8,000 or $12,000. For someone like Judas – who would have been living on next to nothing for the past two years – it must have seemed a considerable sum for one kiss. So he betrayed his Lord, his calling, and himself, for money.

In the parable of the sower, Jesus taught that some 'are choked by the cares and riches and pleasures of life, and their fruit does not mature' (Luke 8:14). Judas was one of those who was choked with spectacular results. Sadly, many today show that Jesus' words are still true. The love of riches – the opposite of generosity – chokes the life out of too many believers. They remain alive, but are without fruit.

A small boy

The small boy of John 6:9 is a startling contrast to Judas. We don't know his name. As far as we know, this is his only appearance on the pages of Scripture. But what an example he is to us all!

> This packed lunch stands as a rebuke to all who think that their gift is too small to make any difference

The boy is one in a crowd of thousands listening to Jesus when suddenly there is a need. Philip estimates that 200 denarii is required – at least £12,000 or $18,000 – to feed all the hungry people. It's a massive need. And this small boy offers his packed lunch as a contribution!

Andrew comments, 'What are they among so many!' Isn't this precisely what we think when we know that a large sum of money is needed and we can make only a tiny contribution. *Mammon* tells us that our gift is too small to make any difference. *Mammon* presses us to hang on to our money because it's of no consequence compared to the need. *Mammon* will do *anything* to stop us giving!

But the boy gave the best that he had. He gave all that he had. It didn't seem much to Andrew, but it was a pretty big sacrifice to the boy. He would go without lunch for Jesus.

And Jesus used the gift in a way which echoes down the

centuries. This packed lunch stands as a rebuke to all those who think that their gift is too small to make any difference.

We never know what Jesus will do with our gifts. Like the man in 2 Kings 4:42-44, we would be amazed if we could see the miracles that God achieves through our sacrificial giving.

A poor widow

This lady is one of the greatest biblical givers. We don't know her name, but her story – in Mark 12:41-44 & Luke 21:1-4 – teaches us a vital lesson about giving.

Jesus was doing something we would not admit to doing. He was watching what people were putting in the offering and was carefully assessing the spirit in which they gave!

'He sat down opposite the treasury, and watched the multitude putting money into the treasury. Many rich people put in large sums. And a poor widow came, and put in two small coins, which make a penny. And he called his disciples to him, and said to them. "Truly, I say to you, this poor widow has put in more than all those who are contributing to the treasury. For they contributed out of their abundance, but she out of her poverty has put in everything she had, her whole living" (Mark 12:41-44).'

Jesus was saying that this woman's two small coins – the least valuable coins of her day – were worth more than all the contributions of all the other people added together!

How can that be? It's simple. God doesn't measure what we give, he measures what

> God doesn't measure what we give to him, he measures what we keep back for ourselves. He looks at the percentage we give rather than at the actual amount

we keep back for ourselves. To put it another way, God looks at the percentage we give rather than at the actual amount we contribute.

This is a revolutionary truth – and begins to explain the miracle of the loaves. The boy's gift had looked small on earth. But – because he'd given all he had – it was enormous in heaven. Jesus made the lunch appear as large on earth as it really was in heaven. He enabled the people to see and benefit from the real size of the boy's gift.

This story should change the way we treat people in meetings – and revolutionize the way we count offerings!

People who seem to give little may actually be giving the most! Those who appear to donate large gifts may really be giving only a tiny amount. We have no need to worry about contributing only a small sum of money – *if it's all we have*. God will use it and bless us in a quite awesome way.

The leper

We've noted that Jesus accepted gifts and asked for hospitality. We've seen him commend people who give and reject those who won't. We've read his promises of heavenly treasure for those who give generously. However the gospels introduce only one person whom Jesus actually *ordered* to make a gift.

Matthew 8:1-4, Mark 1:40-44 & Luke 5:12-14 report Jesus' encounter with 'a man full of leprosy'. Jesus healed the man without any conditions, but after the miracle he ordered the man to give. Jesus didn't promise to heal the man *if* he gave. He healed him – end of statement. *Then* he ordered him to make the right offering.

Saying 'thank you' to God isn't enough. Gratitude needs to be expressed in gifts as well

Jesus told him to 'go and show yourself to the priest, and make an offering for your cleansing, as Moses commanded, for a proof to the people' (Luke 5:14). The offering Jesus referred to is described in Leviticus 14:1-32.

88

It was a considerable size: verses 1-20 list what had to be given by most people, and verses 21-32 record the special arrangements for the poor.

There were two reasons for making the offering. To thank God for the healing, and to show people that the sufferer had been healed. It's part of the biblical principle that saying 'thank you' to God isn't enough. Gratitude needs to be expressed in gifts as well.

Summary of principles

So what have we learnt about giving and receiving from Jesus' teaching and from his encounters with people?

By now we should have grasped hold of giving's vital importance, and be able to see its strategic place in our spiritual battle with the powers of the enemy.

Here are some more principles to help us remember what we've learnt in this chapter.

1) *Mammon* – money, wealth, riches – is an evil spiritual power which is always attempting to enslave us.

2) Giving is the basic fruit of repentance.

3) Giving is part of beginning to follow Jesus.

4) We should never charge for ministry.

5) Giving to people is giving to God. Ignoring the needy is ignoring God.

6) Our giving breaks the power of *mammon* and earns us heavenly treasure.

7) We should expect to receive astonishing blessing from God when we give to everyone who asks us – especially the selfish and ungrateful.

8) We should give secretly if we want a heavenly reward.

9) We shall give hospitality to God's servants and the needy.

10) We should release people from their debts to us before asking God to release us from our financial debts.

11) We shall expect to receive basic food and debt release from God.

12) Giving is the essence of worship.

13) God measures what we keep not what we give.

14) God can use sacrificial small gifts to achieve far more than we ever dream possible.

15) We should always thank God with a gift as well as with words.

THE GIVING EARLY CHURCH

When we think of the early church we tend to remember the astonishing growth, the people's boldness, the awesome miracles, and the terrible opposition. We think of Peter in prison, Stephen being stoned, Paul on trial, Ananias being brave, and the crowds who flocked to touch an apostle's apron. We don't often think about the human giving which financed this great move of God's Spirit.

But that's what we're going to do now. We're going to comb the book of Acts for giving. We're going to examine the biblical record of those first thirty years to see what we can learn about giving. We'll look for Christian people who gave, and we'll try to grasp why and what they gave. We'll see how they implemented the principles we've discovered, and we will watch out for any results of their giving. Of course we won't be able to see their *heavenly* treasure, but there might be some interesting *earthly* consequences.

The story of the early church begins with Jesus' last instructions to his disciples just before his triumphant return to heaven. Matthew 28:16-20 records his great commission. 'All authority in heaven and on earth has been given to me. Go therefore and make disciples of all nations, baptizing them in the name of the Father and of the Son and of the Holy Spirit, teaching them to observe all that I have commanded you. And lo, I am with you always, to the close of the age.'

The eleven apostles were told to teach the new disciples to observe *all* Jesus' instructions. Not to obey only some of them, but to keep all of them. As Jesus taught more about money than anything other than the kingdom, we must realize that Jesus meant his financial teaching to apply to all future disciples – to us.

They could not possibly witness accurately if they ignored or misrepresented Jesus' teaching about money

In Acts 1:8, Jesus' last words were the promise that the apostles would be his *witnesses* to the end of the earth. This meant that they had a duty to bear witness – by their words and actions – to *the whole* of Jesus' teaching and life.

They could not possibly witness accurately if they ignored or misrepresented Jesus' teaching about money. As we've seen, Jesus' teaching about *mammon* and giving was simply too large a part of his ministry – too high on the divine list of priorities – for the early church to distort it or downgrade it.

The gift they received

We've seen that the Bible starts and finishes with a fantastic gift from God to men and women. So it shouldn't surprise us to realize that the Bible's account of the early church also begins with a great gift from God. Once again, our study of giving opens with the all-giving God showing his generosity.

Acts 2 describes God's gift of his Spirit on that day of Pentecost. 'They were all filled with the Holy Spirit and began to speak in other tongues, as the Spirit gave them utterance.' God gave them himself. He gave them his Spirit. He blessed them with power. He blessed them with the gift of the ability to express themselves clearly and authoritatively. He blessed them with the gift of speaking in languages which they had not learnt. He blessed them with the gift of prophesy. And he gave all these blessings freely, without any pre-conditions, to people who'd deserted and denied his Son only a few weeks before.

The first results

Peter preached to the crowd to explain what had happened. When he had revealed the truth about Jesus, Peter's listeners were cut to the heart. They asked, '"What shall we do?" Peter said to them, "Repent, and be baptized every one of you in the name of Jesus Christ for the forgiveness of your sins; and you shall receive the gift of the Holy Spirit (Acts 2:37-38)."'

Peter went on to testify 'with many other words and exhorted them, saying, "Save yourselves from this crooked generation (2:40)."' He told them to repent – John the Baptist showed us what this means. And Peter told them to get free of a generation which was crooked.

In the light of all Jesus' teaching, Peter probably spelt out some of Jesus' financial principles to the people. It's likely that he clarified what he'd meant by *repent* and *crooked*. And surely he explained the practical difference that salvation would mean to their lives.

We don't know exactly what Peter said, but he spoke in the power of the Spirit and about three thousand people received his words and were baptized that day. They were the direct consequence of God's gift.

Three thousand converts were the direct consequence of God's gift

What happened at Pentecost is the first hint of a new giving principle which we'll see throughout Acts – that gifts

> Giving isn't just a weapon which breaks the power of *mammon*, it's also a magnet that attracts people to Christ

and giving mean growth. God gave his gift. And thousands of people who saw it turned to the Giver.

It's obvious. Most people are attracted by generous people and repelled by misers. So it's likely that people will be drawn when we give generously like God. This means that giving is not just a spiritual weapon which breaks the power of *mammon*, it's also a spiritual magnet which attracts people to Christ.

The giving community

Acts 2:42-47 describes what happened to these new converts. These verses prove that their repentance was evidenced by a change in their financial behavior, and that giving was central to lives which had been saved from a crooked generation.

'All who believed were together and had all things in common; and they sold their possessions and goods and distributed them to all, as any had need.'

The power of *mammon* had been broken in their lives, so their attitude to their possessions had changed. They had moved from thinking that they *owned* their wealth to believing that they were *stewards* of their wealth.

When they saw needs, they used their wealth to meet them. Notice that they gave 'as any had need'. They didn't give foolishly, lavishly or excessively. They simply met the needs.

Did this make them unhappy? Were they the laughing stock of Jerusalem? No! The Bible reports that 'they partook of food with glad and generous hearts, praising God and having favor with all the people' (2:46-47). Their new-found generosity made them cheerful, and it greatly impressed other people.

In Acts 2:47, we see a second example of the principle that *giving means growth*. 'The Lord added to their number day by day those who were being saved.' Only a dishonest person can read these verses and say that the people's giving was irrelevant to the church's growth. Throughout Acts, the believers' generosity is inseparable from the church's increase – and from mighty God-given miracles.

> Believers' generosity can't be separated from church growth and mighty God-given miracles

Generous leaders

Acts 2:43 is the verse which introduces us to all the astonishing miracles recorded in Acts. We know the wonderful stories so well that sometimes we don't read all the details. In this chapter, I want to show how the gift of miracles is often set in the context of believers' generosity.

Acts 3:1-9 describes a healing miracle in detail. We're not going to examine the story for healing principles, rather we're looking for anything that it teaches about giving.

As Peter and John were going to pray, a man who had been lame from birth was begging from people entering the temple. The man asked them for money. Peter's reply should transfix us. 'I have no silver and gold, but I give you what I have. In the name of Jesus Christ of Nazareth, walk.'

There are three important giving principles here.

[1] Peter and John didn't ignore the beggar. They didn't walk past him like so many believers do today. They stopped, listened, loved – and acted.

[2] Peter and John didn't have any money! They can't have been lying or surely God wouldn't have honored their words as he did. The most probable explanation is that they really didn't have any money because they'd given it all away in the generosity described by Acts 2:43-47.

[3] They were prepared to give the beggar *all* that they had. 'I give you what I have.' What a statement! Don't stare only at the miracle of healing, concentrate also on this wonderful generosity. Recognize that it was Peter's readiness to give what he had to a beggar which God honored in this life-changing miracle.

'I give you what I have'

I've often wondered what would have happened if Peter and John had some cash in their pockets. But because they had given everything, they were able to give even more!

Generous people

Acts 4:32-35 describes the believers' generous spirit. 'No one said that any of the things which he possessed was his own, but they had everything in common. And with great power the apostles gave their testimony to the resurrection of the Lord Jesus, and great grace was upon them all. There was not a needy person among them, for as many as were possessors of lands or houses sold them, and brought the proceeds of what was sold and laid it at the apostles' feet; and distribution was made to each as any had need.'

We shouldn't lift the apostles' powerful testimony out of the context of this amazing generosity. This giving was part of their testimony to the resurrection of Jesus. People could only give like this because of Jesus! Their generosity was part of the proof that Jesus was alive.

There's a principle here that we've seen before: giving to people should meet their needs, but not anything more. These first Christians still had control over the possessions which God had given to them, but now they had a quite different attitude to them. The apostles didn't take over the peoples' wealth and the believers didn't give all their goods away. They stewarded them for God, using them to meet needs: they decided what to sell and when to sell it.

There is an important 'giving' development in these verses. For the first time, Christians organized their giving so that their gifts were used more efficiently. Instead of giving only to the poor personally, believers *also* gave to a central fund which directed their giving to the most needy. This ensured that some people didn't get too much and that others weren't overlooked.

In the Old Testament, the people's tithes in every third year were collected together in each town to create a common store from which the poor could be fed. The early church followed this pattern. The people gave their gifts into a common fund which was administered by the leaders so that 'distribution was made to each as any had need'.

Obviously this fund was used to provide for those who had no income because they were ministering, as well as for widows, elderly folk and other people unable to work. This development is crucial – because it helps us begin to relate the principles we see in scripture to our complex lives today.

> The people gave their gifts into a common fund which was distributed by the leaders to those in need

A giving contrast

Luke – the author of Acts – makes many deliberate 'giving' contrasts throughout Luke and Acts. We've seen him take us straight from the rich young ruler to Zacchaeus, and now he compares Barnabas with Ananias and Sapphira.

Barnabas sold one of his fields and gave the proceeds to the apostles for the common fund. But 'a man named Ananias with his wife Sapphira sold a piece of property, and with his wife's knowledge he kept back some of the proceeds, and brought only a part and laid it at the apostles' feet' (Acts 5:1-2). Ananias was still in the grip of *mammon*.

He wanted the esteem of giving generously, but he couldn't bear to part with all the proceeds of his property.

Peter makes it plain, in verse four, that Ananias was under no obligation to sell the property. It would have been entirely in order for him to give only part of the proceeds. But he lied. He wanted earthly acclaim *and* earthly treasure. Ananias couldn't admit that he wouldn't give all.

> He wanted earthly acclaim *and* earthly treasure. He couldn't admit that he wouldn't give all

The deaths of Ananias and Sapphira in Acts 5:5-11 are a fearsome warning to all who want their giving publicized, and to all who give for selfish motives. Just as Israel's story begins with God's rejection of Cain for giving less than his best, so the church's history begins with God's rejection of a couple whose giving was unacceptable.

This story shows that God takes our giving *very* seriously. He's watching us, like Jesus watched the widow at the treasury. It may have seemed to some that Ananias gave a large amount. But God was counting what he kept back!

Miraculous blessing

Acts 5:12-16 describes some miraculous blessings which, again, are set in a context of generosity – as well as against a backdrop of prayer and unity. 'Now many signs and wonders were done among the people.' 'More than ever believers were added to the Lord, multitudes both of men and women.' 'The people also gathered from the towns around Jerusalem, bringing the sick and those afflicted with unclean spirits, and they were all healed.'

Isn't that wonderful! We all ache to experience something like this in our own localities. But we need to recognize that God gave miracles and growth to the church at a time when believers were giving so much to others themselves.

Giving problems

The Bible doesn't hide the problems of the people it describes. We all know how difficult it is to allocate funds fairly. There are always people who want us to meet different needs from the ones that we've chosen.

Acts 6:1-7 describes the early church's problem. Their numbers had grown so much that – despite the common fund – one group of widows were being overlooked in the daily food distribution. There was simply too much for the apostles to do. They couldn't preach *and* distribute the resources fairly. So the apostles decided to delegate.

'Brethren, pick out seven men of good repute, full of the Spirit and of wisdom, whom we may appoint to this duty. But we will devote ourselves to prayer and to the ministry of the word.'

They solved their problem by organizing themselves in a godly fashion. They chose seven men to be jointly responsible for the finances. These weren't men who necessarily had financial experience, rather they were men who were full of the Spirit and wisdom. These seven 'deacons' had the task of ensuring that the people's giving was properly administered.

They solved the problem by organizing themselves in a godly fashion. They chose seven Spirit-filled men to be jointly responsible for the finances

We should expect what happened next. 'The word of God increased, and the number of the disciples multiplied greatly in Jerusalem.' God blesses with growth when we give generously *and* when giving is administered in a godly way.

Free gifts

A persecution began and the Jerusalem believers were scattered. One of the deacons – Philip – escaped north to Samaria, where vast numbers of people were converted by his preaching and by the miracles God worked through him.

Simon, a prominent local magician, believed and was baptized. But he didn't understand God's giving principles.

Acts 8:14-24 describes his encounter with Peter. 'When Simon saw that the Spirit was given through the laying on of the apostles' hands, he offered them money.' Peter replied with fury, 'Your silver perish with you, because you thought you could obtain the gift of God with money!' Read verses 21-23 and see the strong language Peter used to rebuke Simon. Clearly, he thought it awful that someone should try to buy God's gift.

Simon didn't realize that he was doing anything wrong. His suggestion was normal in the world

Simon was a new believer. He didn't realize that he was doing anything wrong. What he was suggesting was normal in the 'crooked' world. So today, there are always 'believers' who suggest sensible financial practices which are opposed to God's giving principles. They mean well, but they're as wrong as Simon.

Generous saints

Luke – the author of Acts – views generosity as the key test of a person's spirituality. In his gospel, the only personal information he gives about the people he describes is whether or not they are generous. John the Baptist (3:10-11), the Capernaum centurion (7:5-6), Joanna and Susanna (8:1-3), Zacchaeus (19:8-10) the treasury widow (21:1-4) and Joseph (23:50-54) all illustrate how Luke consistently commends those believers who give generously.

It's the same in Acts. Luke constantly puts God's

spotlight on a person's generosity. He knows that God is watching our giving to see what we keep back for ourselves.

Luke constantly puts God's spotlight on a person's generosity. He knows that God is watching our giving to see what we keep back

In Acts 9:36-39 he describes Dorcas as 'full of good works and acts of charity'. When Peter arrived, 'all the widows stood beside him weeping, and showing tunics and other garments which Dorcas made while she was with them'. There's no suggestion that Dorcas was wealthy – she doesn't appear to have owned a house – but she was generous with the little she had.

Then, in Acts 10:1-2, he introduces Cornelius, 'a centurion of what was known as the Italian Cohort, a devout man who feared God with all his household, gave alms liberally to the people, and prayed constantly to God'.

Cornelius was a wealthy person with an important position in society. He is commended because he gave generously. In fact Cornelius was told that his prayers and alms had 'ascended as a memorial before God' (10:4).

We must never forget that prayer is vital. But, equally, we must realize that there's no integrity in asking God to meet needs when he's already given us the resources to meet them ourselves! God wants us to pray

There's no integrity in asking God to meet needs when he's given us the resources to meet them ourselves

and give like Cornelius. Both these spiritual disciplines are required, we shouldn't choose between them.

The hospitality issue

Cornelius was used by God to bring about two fundamental changes in the early church. Despite God's pleas for Jews to treat strangers well, none of them would enter a non-Jew's home. They believed it would make them unclean.

This idea had been absorbed into the church – which was comprised then of only Jews. There was no mixing with Gentiles – with non-Jews. The tensions about the daily food distribution had been between Hebrew-speaking Jewish believers and Greek-speaking Jewish believers. Nobody in the early church thought that a Gentile could be a disciple.

In Acts 10:1-8, God spoke to Cornelius through an angel, and told him to invite Simon Peter to his home! Cornelius knew this would breach Jewish practice, yet he preferred to obey God. Meanwhile, in 10:9-29, God was speaking to Peter in a puzzling vision which he could not understand.

Since Cornelius there are no excuses for placing limits on our hospitality

It seemed to Peter that God was telling him to change his views about food. Three times a voice said to him, 'What God has cleansed, you must not call common'.

While Peter was considering the vision 'the Spirit said to him, "Behold, three men are looking for you. Rise and go down, and accompany them without hesitation; for I have sent them" (10:20)'.

Peter went with them to Cornelius' house and explained that God had shown him not to call anybody common or unclean. Peter spoke about Jesus and was amazed when the Holy Spirit fell on the Gentiles listening to him (10:34-48). They all spoke in tongues and praised God!

This news soon reached the believers in Jerusalem, who asked Peter, 'Why did you go to uncircumcised men and eat with them? (11:3)'. When the disciples heard Peter's report 'they glorified God, saying "Then to the Gentiles also God has granted repentance unto life" (11:18)'.

This was a decisive moment in the church's development.

Since Peter's visit to Cornelius there have been no excuses for placing limits on our hospitality. We should be eager to eat and mix with those who are outside our racial or social group *and* with those outside the church.

Sadly, there are many believers today who act like the believers before Cornelius. They never eat with anyone outside their own group.

Giving to those far away

Acts 11:27-30 records another important development in giving. Barnabas and Saul were teaching Gentile believers in Syrian Antioch – almost 400 miles north of Jerusalem.

Some prophets visited them. 'One of them named Agabus stood up and foretold by the Spirit that there would be a great famine over all the world.'

The prophets didn't tell the Antioch believers what to do, they simply acquainted them with a forthcoming need. The disciples decided for themselves to meet this need.

'The disciples determined, every one according to his ability, to send relief to the brethren who lived in Judea. And they did so, sending it to the elders by the hand of Barnabas and Saul.'

Until this point in time, giving had been for local needs. Tithes, sacrifices and offerings had all been for local leaders and nearby needy. Now the believers accepted that they had a responsibility for the needy far away, that they should also give to those whom they could not see and had never met.

Until this point in time, giving had been for local needs. Now the believers accepted that they had a responsibility for the needy far away

This is a vitally important principle for us today. We know about so many needs overseas – and in parts of our own countries which we choose not to visit. Most of us have the resources to help meet some of these needs. But do we? How much do we keep back for ourselves?

Interestingly, it's these Antioch givers who 'were for the first time called Christians'. If we want to wear their label, perhaps we should give like them too.

Profiting from ministry

After Saul (Paul) and Barnabas had returned from delivering the offering to Jerusalem, the Antioch Christians sent them off on a ministry tour. From this point on, Acts follows Saul and records his journeys and adventures as God used him to spread the good news throughout the known world.

We saw that Jesus' travels were financed both by a group of committed supporters who gave generously out of their own resources, and by people who provided hospitality when it was needed or requested.

Paul does not appear always to have followed Jesus' example. Rather than always staying with believers, he often paid for lodgings in the towns he visited. Instead of receiving gifts of money from the churches he was visiting, he preferred to depend on a group of committed partners in Macedonia.

Acts 16:15 describes Paul and Silas accepting hospitality from Lydia in Philippi. But that was exceptional. Lydia would not accept a refusal, and she seems to have become one of his partners – who were mainly based in Philippi.

The riot in Philippi provides us with the context which explains Paul's reluctance to benefit personally from his ministry. Acts 16:16-24 describes his encounter with a slave-girl who 'had a spirit of divination and brought her owners much gain by soothsaying'.

At that time – and still today – many people made their fortunes from religion. So the girl's owners were furious when Paul cast the evil spirit out of her. 'When her owners saw that their hope of gain was gone, they seized Paul and Silas and dragged them into the market place.'

Paul did not want anyone to be able to say that he was preaching for money. He didn't want people to have a chance of thinking that he was benefiting from his ministry. He knew that Jesus had sent the twelve out to preach, to heal and to 'give without pay'. So Paul did everything possible to ensure that this was how he lived and ministered.

> Paul did not want anyone to be able to say that he was preaching for money. He didn't want people to think that he was benefiting from his ministry

He didn't want to give anyone a reason for rejecting the good news. It was much too important for that!

Unrighteous mammon

Acts 19:11-20 records a remarkable story which reminds us of the spiritual power behind money.

Paul had been in Ephesus for over two years, and God had blessed his work greatly with many miracles. A group of traveling exorcists tried to cast an evil spirit out of a sufferer and were badly mauled by the demon-possessed man. The news got out and 'became known to all the residents of Ephesus, both Jews and Greeks. Fear fell upon them all, and the name of the Lord Jesus was extolled.'

Clearly this dramatic incident caused the believers to talk about demon possession and to discuss God's way of releasing people. Acts 19:18-20 describes what happened.

'Many also of those who were now believers came, confessing and divulging their practices. And a number of those who practiced magic arts brought their books together and burned them in the sight of all. They counted the value of them and found it came to fifty thousand pieces of silver.'

There must have been terrible needs in the area. There would have been countless people who were hungry and homeless. The work of spreading the gospel needed to be financed. Fifty thousand pieces of silver was a vast fortune. Think what such a huge sum could have been used to accomplish! So why were the books burnt and not sold?

Missionary work needed to be financed. There were countless hungry and homeless. So why weren't the books sold and the proceeds used for good causes?

We saw in the Old Testament that Jews couldn't sacrifice anything which had been unlawfully obtained. We noted that – as part of their commitment to Jesus – the first four disciples chose not to benefit from a bumper catch of fish. We learnt from Jesus that there's a spiritual force behind wealth, and that objects bearing Caesar's mark must be given to Caesar.

When we add these principles together we can see that these evil books belonged to Satan. They had his mark on them: he was the force behind them. They couldn't be used as an offering for God. It's blasphemous even to suggest such a terrible thing.

Yet today there would be those who'd argue that the books should be sold and the money given away. Such people are blind to spiritual forces – they don't recognize that there are evil spirits behind evil objects.

Jesus told us that he'd come to destroy the works of the enemy, and that we were to trample the enemy underfoot. So we must not use the proceeds of evil to support the work of the kingdom *or* to help feed and clothe the poor.

Giving to the poor is giving to God. Would God want money which had been tainted by Satan?

We should remember what happened to Cain and to Ananias when they offered God unacceptable gifts!

> We mustn't use the proceeds of evil to support the work of the kingdom *or* to help the poor

Acts 19:20 tells us what happened after the bonfire. 'The word of the Lord grew and prevailed mightily.' It's the same principle that we've seen so many times before in Acts: sacrificial giving means growth. When will we learn?

Money trouble

I'm sure that most readers have thought of Paul's famous principle: 'the love of money is the root of all evils'. We haven't reached Paul's letters yet, but some of the incidents we're examining in Acts must have contributed to Paul's feelings about the grip that money has on people.

Luke introduces the worst New Testament riot with this understatement in 19:23. 'About that time there arose no little stir concerning the Way.' Money was behind the row.

A silversmith called Demetrius thought that the gospel was losing him income. Fewer people were buying the trinkets he made of the false-God Artemis. He told his colleagues, 'Men you know that from this business we have our wealth...Paul has persuaded and turned away a considerable company of people...And there is danger that this trade of ours may come into disrepute (19:23-27).'

Demetrius was enslaved to *mammon*. He didn't want to lose any of his income. So he instigated a riot which meant that Paul had to leave town.

> Money was behind the row. Fewer people were buying trinkets of the false-God Artemis

The gospel always puts some people out of business, and I guarantee that there'll always be trouble over money and giving. This means we must

We must be careful that our thinking about money, and our motives for asking and giving, are right before God

always be most careful that we are thinking about money in God's way. We need to double-check that our motives for asking and for giving are pleasing to God.

Paul's farewell

The trouble at Ephesus convinced Paul that terrible afflictions and persecution lay ahead of him. When he was traveling to Jerusalem, he had to summon the leaders of the Ephesian Christians to meet him in Miletus because it was too dangerous for him to enter Ephesus.

Acts 20:17-37 records Paul's farewell sermon to the Ephesians whom he'd served for over two years. His closing remarks were about money.

'I coveted no one's silver or gold or apparel. You yourselves know that these hands ministered to my necessities, and to those who were with me. In all things I have shown you that by so toiling one must help the weak, remembering the words of the Lord Jesus, how he said, "It is more blessed to give than to receive". And when he had spoken thus, he knelt down and prayed with them all.'

Of all the topics he could have spoken about in farewell, he chose giving. Instead of urging them to preach the gospel, he reminded them not to covet wealth and to work hard so that they could give to the weak. And from all the sayings of Jesus that he could have left with them, he chose 'It is more blessed to give than to receive'.

Remember the words of the Lord Jesus, "It is more blessed to give than to receive"

Giving was so high on Paul's priorities for Christian believers that he made it the last thing he said to his disciples. Whenever they remembered Paul in the future, they would recall this farewell sermon on giving.

This saying of Jesus doesn't appear in the gospels. But it wonderfully encapsulates the teaching of Jesus and Paul – and the life of the early church. They knew that giving brought far more happiness than receiving – and meant great blessing. They understood that giving caused growth and was God's way for his children. They'd grasped the truth that generous giving broke the power of the enemy and was the best way to live. The members of the early church were generous givers like their all-giving God – it was one of the secrets of their astonishing success.

Summary of principles

Again, I've summarized what we've seen in Acts into the following key principles. They will help us to remember the important truths we've learnt in this chapter.

1) Giving is part of our witness to the truth about Jesus.

2) Giving communities are blessed with church growth – generosity attracts people to Jesus.

3) God works miracles through giving communities.

4) Our giving needs to be organized effectively by Spirit-filled leaders.

5) God's way of giving doesn't make any sense to the world – and vice versa.

6) We should put no limits on our hospitality.

7) We have a responsibility for the needy far away.

8) We should not profit from Christian ministry.

9) Money causes problems.

10) It is more blessed to give than to receive.

NEW TESTAMENT GIVING PRINCIPLES

We began this book by gazing at our all-giving God. We thought about him as Creator and Redeemer, and realized that giving is at the root of his divine character. However, we've been looking at human giving for the last four chapters, and it's easy to forget basic principles.

When we search the rest of the New Testament for teaching about giving, we see that most passages are about God and his gifts. The pages from Romans to Revelation are peppered with descriptions of God's generous giving, lists of his gifts, and reminders of his grace and mercy.

We give because that's what God does. We are generous because he has given us everything we are and everything we have. Human giving – even at its best – can be only the palest reflection of God's giving.

Before we press on with more teaching about *our* giving, let's remind ourselves about *his* giving. If God's loving actions aren't the basis for our behavior, we might drift into lifeless legalism.

Here are five important passages about God's blessings to launch us into the New Testament teaching about giving.

'God has endured with much patience the vessels of wrath

made for destruction, in order to make known the *riches of his glory* for the vessels of mercy, which he has prepared beforehand for glory, even us (Romans 9:22-23).'

'You are not lacking in *any spiritual gift*, as you wait for the revealing of our Lord Jesus Christ; who will sustain you to the end, guiltless (1 Corinthians 1:7-8).'

May God give you 'a spirit of wisdom and revelation in the knowledge of him, having the eyes of your hearts enlightened, that you may know what is the hope to which he has called you – what are *the riches of his glorious inheritance* in the saints, and what is the immeasurable greatness of his power in us who believe, according to the working of his great might (Ephesians 1:17-19)'.

'But God, who is rich in mercy, out of the great love with which he loved us, even when we were dead through our trespasses, made us alive together with Christ (by grace you have been saved). He raised us up with him, and made us sit with him in the heavenly places in Christ Jesus, that in the coming ages he might show the *immeasurable riches of his grace in kindness toward us in Christ Jesus.* For by grace you have been saved through faith; and this is not your own doing, it is the gift of God (Ephesians 2:4-8).'

> **These verses are just the smallest mouthful of the mighty feast of God's generosity described in the New Testament**

'His divine power has granted to us *all things that pertain to life and godliness* – through the knowledge of him who called us to his own glory and excellence – by which he has granted to us *his precious and very great promises* (2 Peter 1:3-4).'

These verses are just the smallest mouthful of the mighty feast of God's generosity described in the letters of the New Testament. Unless we're gripped by God's amazing giving, unless we are dazzled by his grace and mercy, we'll never begin to understand why loving, grateful generosity should be the dominant feature of our lives.

> **Unless we're gripped by God's amazing giving, we won't understand why loving generosity should dominate our lives**

Hardships and joy

The repeated descriptions of the believers' hardships and sufferings stand out when we scan the pages of the New Testament letters for examples of human giving.

The early church's extraordinary giving may have contributed to their fantastic growth. Their generosity may have been blessed by God with mighty miracles. But they didn't have an easy life.

Poverty, persecution, opposition, imprisonment, exile and martyrdom were their lot – and deep, deep joy! The giving of the first Christians may have earnt them unlimited heavenly treasure and wonderful spiritual blessings on earth, but it didn't bring them material riches. However, it did make them cheerful, contented and incredibly fulfilled.

Mammon always insists that giving will make us miserable. We must never believe him. It's a lie! It's acting as a miser which makes us *miserable*.

There's a deep biblical principle that God's glory is only ever seen at the place of sacrifice. If we want to taste his glory, we have to live sacrificially.

> **Mammon insists that giving will make us miserable. Don't believe him. It's a lie!**

Before we examine closely the New Testament teaching about giving, here are five passages to remind us of the circumstances that the first Christians faced – and in which they lived so generously.

'To the present hour we hunger and thirst. We are ill-clad and buffeted and homeless. We labor, working with our own hands. When reviled, we bless. When persecuted, we endure. When slandered, we try to reconciliate. We have become, and are now, as the refuse of the world, the off-scouring of all things (1 Corinthians 4:10-13).'

'As servants of God we commend ourselves in every way: through great endurance in afflictions, hardships, calamities, beatings, imprisonments, tumults, labors, watching and hunger; by purity, knowledge, forbearance, kindness, the Holy Spirit, genuine love, truthful speech, and the power of God...We are treated as impostors, and yet are true...as sorrowful, yet always rejoicing; as poor, yet making many rich; as having nothing, and yet possessing everything (2 Corinthians 6:4-10).'

'For the sake of Christ, I am content with weaknesses, insults, hardships, persecutions, and calamities; for when I am weak, then I am strong (2 Corinthians 12:10).'

'Share in the sufferings as a good soldier of Christ Jesus (2 Timothy 2:3).'

'Count it all joy, my brethren when you meet various trials, for you know that the testing of your faith produces steadfastness. And let steadfastness have its full effect, that you may be perfect and complete, lacking in nothing (James 1:2).'

> Count it all joy when you meet various trials, for you know that the testing of your faith produces steadfastness

We won't grasp the significance of the New Testament teaching about generosity until we appreciate this background of hardships and difficulties.

Biblical giving principles are not a recipe for instant earthly prosperity, but they are God's way to blessing and joy. When we give in his way we are on a certain path to peace and maturity – we're following his route to righteousness. Never forget, giving is the highway to heavenly treasure.

Good works

There's a relentless New Testament emphasis on the importance of good works. Far too many evangelical believers are so busy insisting that good works can't save us, that they overlook all the verses which insist that we've been saved *to do* good works.

Paul's teaching in Romans 2:6-10 – and many of Jesus' parables – shows that our heavenly reward is related to the good works we've performed. 1 John 3:16-18 clearly demonstrates that good works are an aspect of giving.

> If any has the world's goods and sees his brother in need, yet closes his heart against him, how does God's love abide in him? Let us not love in word or speech but in deed and truth

'By this we know love, that he laid down his life for us; and we ought to lay down our lives for the brethren. But if any has the world's goods and sees his brother in need, yet closes his heart against him, how does God's love abide in him? Little children, let us not love in word or speech but in deed and in truth.'

These words are pointed at us. We live in an age when most North American and Western European believers are well aware of their Third World brothers and sisters' acute needs. We are those who 'have the world's goods'.

But do we love our poor Third World brothers in word or in deed? Have we closed our hearts to them? Does God's love abide in us? Or has *mammon* tricked us into thinking that our gift would be too small to make any difference?

Jesus' parable about the Last Judgement, in Matthew 25:31-46, makes it unavoidably clear that our love for God is measured by our practical caring for the poor. If we are believers, good works must feature in our lives.

Godly thinking

Paul reminds us, in Romans 12:1-2, that God's way of living is far removed from the world's normal practices. 'Do not be conformed to this world but be transformed by the renewal of your mind, that you may prove what is the will of God, what is good and acceptable and perfect.'

> A change of thinking comes before a change in behavior. Our giving will be transformed only when we start thinking like God

This verse shows that a change of thinking must come *before* a change in behavior. Our behavior will be transformed only by a revolution in our thinking. Our giving will be changed only when we start to think like God about wealth and financial principles.

That's precisely why I've gone to such lengths in this book to explain *why* we should give. If we give only because someone urges us, there hasn't been a change in our thinking: our giving won't last. And if we give only to get something back for ourselves on this earth, we're still thinking in the world's way, not in God's.

But once we grasp the godly principles involved we'll persist in giving generously for right reasons and pure motives. Remember, the world's ideas about giving are the exact opposite of God's ideas, so there must be a total transformation in our thinking – a complete mental revolution – before we can start giving like God.

That's why it's important that we read and re-read this

book; that we check all the references and fully understand God's giving principles.

I can't think of anything which is more urgent for the kingdom of God in these days than that God's people start to think God's thoughts about giving.

Paul's principles

The apostle Paul dominates our knowledge of the early church. He is the man whom God used to plant so many churches and evangelize so much of the Roman Empire in the thirty years after Christ's return to heaven.

His letters are a major part of the New Testament (though Luke actually contributed more words than Paul), and his ideas must shape our thinking about gifts and giving.

Paul sets out his principles for *accepting gifts* in three main passages: 1 Corinthians 9; 2 Corinthians 11; and 2 Thessalonians 3:6-12.

In 1 Corinthians 9:14, he makes it clear that 'the Lord commanded that those who proclaim the gospel should get their living by the gospel'. From 9:3 to 9:14 he uses example after example to convince his readers that those who serve the church should have their needs met by the church. This follows the Old Testament practice of providing for priests and levites by the people's tithes.

But Paul refused to live like this. 'Nevertheless, we have not made use of this right, but we endure anything rather than put an obstacle in the way of the gospel of Christ (9:12).' 'I have made no use of any of these rights, nor am I writing this to secure any such provision (9:15).'

Preaching the gospel was Paul's one and only priority. If receiving financial gifts meant

> The Lord commanded that those who proclaim the gospel should get their living by the gospel. But Paul refused to live like this

that some people wouldn't listen to him, he wouldn't accept the gifts. If others wouldn't listen because Timothy was uncircumcised, then Timothy had to be circumcised.

> **Too many people think that full-time, fully-paid ministry is the only way forward. But Paul stands out as a shining example of part-time, unpaid ministry**

In 2 Corinthians 11:7-11, Paul explains that he has accepted support from his Macedonian partners in order to serve the Corinthian church. But 2 Thessalonians 3:6-12 reveals his normal practice of refusing to accept gifts from churches where he is ministering.

'We were not idle when we were with you. We did not eat anyone's bread without paying, but with toil and labor we worked night and day, that we might not burden any of you. It was not because we have not that right, but to give you in our conduct an example to imitate.'

Paul knew that he set an example everywhere he went. More than that, he urged people to imitate him and set a pattern for ministry which is vital for us today. Too many people think that the full-time, fully-paid ministry is the only way forward. But Paul stands out as a shining example of part-time ministry.

Paul financed his work by making tents. He didn't depend on the giving of local people. He didn't demand that folk supported his apostolic ministry. Instead he worked when necessary, and accepted gifts when they came.

> **We need an army of people who'll minister like Paul, who'll work to support themselves and not stint on the serving and preaching**

I must have said thousands of times that we're not going to reach the world for Jesus through full-time ministers alone. We need them. We should all give our tithes to release many more people into ministry. But we also need an army of people who will minister like Paul, who'll work to support themselves and *never* stint on the serving and preaching.

Paul proves that to be part-time is not necessarily to be second rate or second best! His principles of financing ministry are still relevant today.

Paul's offerings

If Paul was reluctant to ask for gifts for himself, he was incredibly zealous in collecting gifts of money for others. Paul is the church's first great fund-raiser.

We saw in Acts that he was at Antioch when they gave so generously for famine relief, and that he took the money with Barnabas to Jerusalem. Two other passages describe different occasions when Paul asked for gifts for needy Jewish believers far away in Israel.

In Romans 15:27-29, Paul explains that fund-raising for Jewish believers is the reason why he's not been able to visit the Romans. 'For Macedonia and Achaia have been pleased to make some contribution for the poor among the saints at Jerusalem; they were pleased to do it, for if the Gentiles have come to share in their spiritual blessings, they also ought to be of service to them in material blessings. When therefore I have completed this, and have delivered to them what has been raised, I shall go on by way of you to Spain.'

> Paul argued that Gentile believers owed an eternal spiritual debt to the Jews, and should give to them as some sort of repayment

Although Paul was primarily a preacher and teacher, he spent much of his time urging people to give. It's important we see that his fund-raising was always for the Jews.

Paul argued that Gentile believers owed an eternal

119

spiritual debt to the Jews, and should give gifts to them in repayment. It's for this reason I also believe that giving to the Jews should be the highest priority today for us all.

We must understand the distinction that Paul made. He believed that he had a right to be supported by those to whom he ministered – but he refused to exercise that right. However he frequently asked people to give to the Jews – their needs mattered more to him than his own.

As well as asking people to give to special large offerings for the Jews, Paul often urged believers to make generous giving a central part of their lives.

For example, in Romans 12 he writes: 'he who contributes, in liberality; he who gives aid, with zeal; he who does acts of mercy with cheerfulness' (vs 8). 'Contribute to the needs of the saints (vs 13) 'If your enemy is hungry, feed him; if he is thirsty, give him drink (vs 20).'

Give hospitality

In particular, Paul urged his readers to make hospitality a special priority. In Romans 12:13, he told people whom he'd never met to 'practice hospitality'. And in Romans 14 he explained that they were even to invite into their homes those difficult people who have strong views about what they should and should not eat.

The writer to the Hebrews also reminded his readers, 'do not neglect to show hospitality to strangers, for thereby some have entertained angels unawares' (Hebrews 13:1).

Practice hospitality ungrudgingly to one another

And Peter pressed believers to 'practice hospitality ungrudgingly to one another' (1 Peter 4:9).

In an age when there are an ever increasing number of homeless people, and when most Christian homes have a spare room or some empty space, the plea for believers to give hospitality surely needs to be made all over again.

Sometimes it's easy to give 'conscious money' to the needy far away – though God watches what we keep back. Yet *mammon* always makes it hard for us to open our homes to strangers. But what a chance to witness – especially when our deeds are louder than our words.

Give with faith

No look at New Testament giving principles is complete without reading Hebrews 11. This is the most famous chapter in the Bible about faith, and – because we know that our giving is meant to be filled with faith – it helps us to grasp some important truths about faith-filled giving.

God rewards those who seek him

This chapter reminds us that 'without faith it is impossible to please God' (vs 6). It teaches us that God 'rewards those who seek him' (vs 6). And it shows us that faith 'is the assurance of things hoped for, the conviction of things *not* seen' (vs 1).

The writer catalogues the heroes of the Old Testament, offering example after example of what he calls faith. His pen-portraits have three things in common.

[1] They all involve some element of personal sacrifice – either in giving something up or in performing a dangerous task at considerable personal risk.

[2] They all carried out their God-given tasks for two reasons: to please God *and* to obtain a promised reward.

[3] None of them received their reward on earth.

This helps us to see the importance of heavenly rewards. Here are three extracts which show that these heroes all thought the promise of God's blessing was so real and so wonderful that it more than made their sacrifice worthwhile.

'They desire a better country, that is, a heavenly one. Therefore God is not ashamed to be called their God, for he has prepared for them a city (vs 16).'

'He considered abuse suffered for the Christ greater wealth than the treasures of Egypt, for he looked to the reward (vs 26).'

'All these, though well attested by their faith, did not receive what was promised, since God has foreseen something better for us (vs 39).'

Faith is needed when our giving is sacrificial, when God smiles at what we keep back, when our love of heavenly rewards is greater than our love of money

Time and again we come back to the same question. Do we desire heaven more than earth? Do we prefer heavenly treasure to earthly wealth? Do we believe that the rewards for giving God's way are better than cash in our pockets?

There's never any faith involved in keeping hold of possessions which we can see and touch, for faith is 'the conviction of things not seen'. And there's very little faith in giving a tenth or mere token offerings.

Faith is only needed when our giving becomes sacrificial, when God smiles with pleasure at what we keep back, when our love of heavenly rewards and holy promises is much greater than our love of money.

Faith is present when our giving shows that our security is in God and not in maintaining a healthy bank balance

Faith is present when our giving shows that our security is only in God alone and not in maintaining a healthy bank balance.

Hebrews 10:34-35 describes the godly attitude to possessions which all believers should aspire towards. 'You had compassion on prisoners, and you joyfully accepted the plundering of your property since you knew that you yourselves had a better possession and an abiding one. Therefore do not throw away your confidence which has a great reward.'

These first Christians could accept the theft of their property with joy because they knew that they had something eternally better which couldn't be stolen. How much more should we be willing to give our property away! That takes faith, and faith pleases God.

Give respect to the poor

For some people, giving is a way of expressing their feelings of control or superiority. Their charity is a statement of power rather than a gift of love and thankfulness. They are not thinking about a heavenly reward. Instead they are pointing out their status to those they consider inferior.

The New Testament emphasizes that we are to give our respect to the poor. We are to consider them equals. We are not to patronize them

Associate with the lowly and never show partiality to the rich

when we meet them. Paul tells us, 'do not be haughty, but associate with the lowly; never be conceited' (Romans 12:16).

James makes the principle plain. 'Show no partiality as you hold the faith of our Lord Jesus Christ. For if a man with gold rings and in fine clothing comes into your assembly, and a poor man in shabby clothing also comes in, and you pay attention to the one who wears the fine clothing and say "Have a seat here please," while you say to the poor man, "Stand there," or, "Sit at my feet," have you not made distinctions among yourselves, and become judges with evil thoughts?... If you show partiality, you commit sin, and are convicted by the law as transgressors.' (James 2:1-9).

It's one thing to make an offering for the poor in Africa. It's quite another matter to treat rough, unwashed, unkempt visitors to our services as honored guests. Yet that's what James calls us to do. But why should we behave like this?

Firstly, because that's how God behaves. He doesn't judge people by their appearances. He looks on the inside not the outside. He treats all people equally. He doesn't give special seats to the rich or privileges to a favored few.

And, secondly, because Jesus taught that the way we treat 'the least of these' is the way we treat him. If we ignore the poor, we're ignoring God. If we look down on the lowly, we're looking down on God. But when we treat the poor with great respect, we're being respectful to God.

> When we treat the poor with great respect, we're being respectful to God

We must never forget that Christ 'who, though he was in the form of God, did not count equality with God a thing to be grasped, but emptied himself, taking the form of a servant' (Philippians 2:6). Christ is our example in this matter. If he took the form of a servant, we should surely respect those who share that chosen form.

Paul insists that, 'in humility count others better than yourselves' (Philippians 2:3). When we genuinely think like this we will give the poor the respect they deserve – and that is a gift which is more valuable than money.

Tithing

The first Christians still paid their tithes to the Jewish religious leaders and made their sacrifices in the Jerusalem Temple. They did this because they were Jews.

However, when Gentiles were welcomed as believers,

there was some dispute as to which Jewish regulations the Gentiles should keep. Should they be circumcised? Should they pay tithes? Were they bound by all the Jewish laws, none of them, or just a few?

After a conference at Jerusalem, the apostles decided that Gentile believers need abstain only from illicit marriages, anything polluted by idols, and the meat of strangled animals. They didn't have to tithe or be circumcised.

> The Jewish system of tithing was God's way of providing an income for religious leaders and for the poor

We've seen that the Jewish system of tithing was God's way of providing an income for religious leaders and for the poor. And even though we haven't seen the tithing system in the New Testament, we have seen the principle behind the system – that Christian believers should give to the poor *and* to religious leaders.

Paul may not have always claimed the right for himself, but he recognized that those who minister the Gospel should receive income for their work. He makes this especially clear in 1 Timothy 5:17. 'Let the elders who rule well be considered worthy of double honor, especially those who labor in preaching and teaching. The scripture says, "You shall not muzzle an ox when it is treading out the grain," and, "The laborer deserves his wages."'

Somehow we have to find a way of applying these principles to our circumstances today.

> Let the elders who rule well be considered worthy of double honor, especially those who labor in preaching and teaching

It's not good enough for modern church leaders to insist that their members tithe because it's biblical, and then to use those tithes for an unbiblical purpose like erecting and furnishing buildings!

The tithing principle is clear – it's God's way of providing income for men and women who are involved in the different aspects of ministry. It's people first – anything else is extra and voluntary.

Sacrifices

The Gentile believers had a similar problem with sacrifices. Clearly they didn't need to offer sacrifices for their sins any more. But how were they to express their thanks to God? How could they give him a love-gift? How could they offer God sacrifices?

> Too many believers today offer God thankspeaking and thanksinging instead of thanksgiving

Several important New Testament passages answer this question. And it's vital that we grasp the principles involved, for far too many believers today offer God thank*speaking* and thank*singing* instead of thanks*giving*.

Paul urges us 'by the mercies of God, to present your bodies as a living sacrifice, holy and acceptable to God, which is your spiritual worship' (Romans 12:1).

He pleads 'be imitators of God, as beloved children. And walk in love, as Christ loved us and gave himself up for us, a fragrant offering and sacrifice to God (Ephesians 5:1-2).'

These two verses are general teaching about modern sacrifices. But in Philippians 4 Paul explains that a financial gift to him from his partners is actually a sacrifice to God.

This is one of the most revolutionary and important passages about giving in the entire New Testament. In fact it's so crucial to our understanding that I'm going to reproduce it in full.

> A financial gift to Paul from his partners is actually a sacrifice to God

'In the beginning of the gospel, when I left

126

Macedonia, no church entered into partnership with me in giving and receiving except you. For even in Thessalonica you sent me help once and again. Not that I seek the gift; but I seek the fruit which increases to your credit. I have received full payment, and more. I am filled, having received from Ephroditus the gifts you sent, a fragrant offering, a sacrifice acceptable and pleasing to God. And my God will supply every need of yours according to his riches in glory in Christ Jesus (Philippians 4:15-20).'

God had used Paul to bring the believers in Philippi to Christ. So – as an expression of their thanks to God for his gift of salvation – these Macedonian believers became partners with Paul in the work of the gospel.

They remained behind in Philippi as witnesses to the resurrection, but they sent regular financial gifts to Paul which supported his ministry.

Paul classified these gifts as sacrifices to God which were 'acceptable and pleasing' to God. But more than that, Paul promised his partners that – because of their generosity – God would supply every need that they had!

This is what I do today. I encourage those people who've been spiritually blessed by God's ministry in my life to become partners in the work.

My partners stay at home as witnesses to the risen Lord, but send regular financial gifts which enable the gospel to be preached around the world.

This is what I do today. I encourage those people who've been spiritually blessed by God's ministry in my life to become partners in the work

The gifts my partners send, like Paul's, are sacrifices which delight God. And, following Paul, I stand upon the promise of God that he will supply my partners' every need.

Paul never promised that his partners would become

prosperous. But he did promise that 'My God will supply every need of yours according to his riches in glory in Christ Jesus'. Every need means *every* need. It includes health needs, financial needs like debts, employment needs, family needs, and so on.

> Every need means *every* need. It includes health needs, financial needs, employment needs, family needs, and so on

In the final chapter, some of my partners testify how God has blessed them greatly and met their deep needs as they've given sacrificially to this ministry.

Of course Paul isn't saying that the *only* way to offer God sacrifices is to send him money. He is simply making it clear that his partners' committed, regular, loving, thankful giving to him is *the same* as a sacrifice to God.

Hebrews 13:16 repeats this idea, 'Do not neglect to do good and to share what you have, for such sacrifices are pleasing to God'. Giving – when it is sacrificial – is a sacrifice to God personally which brings him great pleasure.

False teachers

There's obviously a danger that some leaders will abuse this teaching and press people to give to them. The New Testament points this out and names such men as false teachers. 2 Peter 2:3 says that 'in their greed they will exploit you'. In every age, there have always been those who have used religion to make themselves rich. These men are servants of *mammon* rather than servants of God.

In 1 Timothy 6 2-13, Paul contrasts true and false teaching. He makes it clear that a teacher's attitude to money is a test of their truth or falsehood.

'There is great gain in godliness with contentment. For we brought nothing into the world, and we cannot take anything out of the world. But if we have food and clothing with these shall we be content. But those who desire to be rich fall into temptation, into a snare, into many senseless and hurtful desires that plunge men into ruin and destruction. For the love of money is the root of all evils; it is through this craving that some have wandered away from the faith and pierced their hearts with many pangs. But as for you, man of God, shun all this.'

> Those who desire to be rich fall into temptation, into a snare, into many senseless and hurtful desires that plunge men into ruin and destruction

Here, Paul urges those of us who would be men and women of God to shun the desire for riches and to embrace godly contentment. Men and women who want to become rich won't want to be generous givers.

Some people pretend to themselves that they want to be rich only so that they can become givers. But they should start giving immediately and remember Jesus' principles.

At the treasury, the widow gave more than the rich men added together. The small boy's lunch was enough to feed thousands of people.

Jesus taught, in Matthew 7:15-20, that we should avoid false prophets who come in 'sheep's clothing but inwardly are ravenous wolves'. Jesus promises that we will know them by their fruits.

He spoke those words in the context of urging his disciples to be contented, to be generous givers, to be servants of God rather than *mammon*. False teachers and false prophets are

> The love of money is the root of all evils; it is through this craving that some have wandered away from the faith

to be avoided, and one of the ways we can recognize them is by their attitude to money. Do they seek it? Do they keep it? Or are they givers like God, like the apostles of old?

Rich Christians

There are some believers who – like Barnabas, Zacchaeus, Mary and Martha – are very affluent. God has blessed them financially in the same way that he has blessed other folk with great intellects or outstanding musical ability.

In 1 Timothy 6:17-19, Paul gives these wealthy Christians their personal instructions. 'As for the rich in this world, charge them not to be haughty, nor to set their hopes on uncertain riches but on God who richly furnishes us with everything we enjoy. They are to do good, to be rich in good deeds, liberal and generous, thus laying up for themselves a good foundation for the future, so that they may take hold of the life which is life indeed.'

Paul does not order them to give all their money away and become poor. Instead he reminds them about their special responsibility to be generous, and warns them about the danger of depending on the wrong sort of riches.

The Bible does not condemn the rich for being rich. Rather it condemns people who won't give generously, and that's a disease which afflicts rich and poor alike.

> You say, 'I am rich and need nothing' not knowing that you are wretched, pitiable and poor. Buy from me gold refined by fire, that you may be truly rich

The church at Laodicea was prosperous, but it was condemned for trusting in the wrong sort of riches – not for being wealthy. 'I will spew you out of my mouth. For you say, I am rich, I have prospered and I need nothing; not knowing that you are wretched, pitiable, poor, blind and naked. Therefore I counsel you to buy from me gold refined by fire, that you may be rich (Revelation 3:15-22).'

As we've seen throughout the Bible, God wants us to desire heavenly treasure more than earthly wealth. It doesn't matter how much earthly wealth we have, so long as we know that it is all dust and ashes compared to the solid gold of heaven *and* that we give it away generously.

Giving to Jewish believers

Chapters eight and nine of 2 Corinthians are packed with more teaching about giving than any other part of the New Testament. In them, Paul urges the Corinthian believers to join his Philippian partners in giving as generously as possible to Jewish believers.

Please read these two awesome chapters now. Read them slowly and carefully. There isn't space to print them in full in this book, but I'm going to pick out some of the highlights because they illustrate and apply all the principles we've been examining in this section.

> Their abundance of joy and extreme poverty have overflowed in a wealth of liberality. They gave according to their means, and beyond their means, of their own free will

Here's Paul's description of his partners' generosity to the Jews. He is not praising them for giving to his ministry, rather he is complimenting them for giving to Jewish believers.

'In a severe test of affliction, their abundance of joy and their extreme poverty have overflowed in a wealth of liberality on their part. For they gave according to their means, as I can testify, and beyond their means, of their own free will, begging us earnestly for the favor of taking part in the relief of the saints.'

Paul doesn't mince his words in urging the Corinthians to give. 'As you excel in everything...see that you excel in this gracious work also.'

He lists three reasons why they should give generously to the Jewish believers.

[1] To prove 'that your love also is genuine'.

[2] To follow the example of Jesus, 'that though he was rich, yet for your sake he became poor'.

[3] To bring equality between the saints, 'as a matter of equality your abundance at the present time should supply their want'.

These three reasons still exist. I believe it is imperative that we take these words to heart and give to the Jews as generously as Paul's partners. This is precisely why helping Jews is such a high priority in this ministry. Is there really any excuse for not giving to the spiritually needy in Israel?

In these chapters, Paul takes pains to explain how he is administering the gift. 'For we aim at what is honorable not only in the Lord's sight but also in the sight of men.' It's vital that our finances are administered carefully today, so nobody can point a finger of accusation at God's people.

> Each must do as he has made up his mind, not reluctantly or under compulsion, for God loves a cheerful giver. And God is able to provide you with every blessing in abundance, so that you always have enough of everything

Paul closes these two chapters on giving to the Jews with a series of pleas and promises. There's no better way of dealing with any controversy about giving than by letting these words sink deep into our minds. There's never been a better fund-raising letter for the Jews than this! Paul's words are still God's principles for us today.

'He who sows sparingly will also reap sparingly, and he who sows bountifully will reap bountifully. Each one must do as he has made up his mind, not reluctantly or under compulsion, for God loves a cheerful giver. And God is able to provide you with every blessing in abundance, so that you always have enough of everything (9:6-9).'

'He who supplies seed to the sower and bread for food will supply and multiply your resources and increase the harvest of your righteousness. You will be enriched in every way for great generosity, which through us will produce thanksgiving to God. For the rendering of this service not only supplies the wants of the saints but also overflows in many thanksgivings to God (9:10-12).'

'Under the test of this service, you will glorify God by your obedience in acknowledging the gospel of Christ, and by the generosity of your contribution for them and for all others; while they long for you and pray for you, because of the surpassing grace of God in you (9:13-14).'

It's easy to be carried away by these great promises. But we must not forget that these blessings are promised to those who will give to the Jews. We shouldn't take these words and apply them to every aspect of giving.

Paul ends his fund-raising letter with a great shout of praise. And our giving will only become the delightful, joyful privilege we've been reading about in the New Testament when the words of his 2 Corinthians 9:15 shout are the main reason for all our giving.

'Thanks be to God for his inexpressible gift!'

GIVING TODAY

Jesus began and ended his public ministry by cleansing the Jerusalem temple. This was a deeply symbolic action which showed that the Messiah had come to purge Israel from its worship of *mammon*.

John 2:15 describes what happened, 'making a whip of cords, he drove them all, with the sheep and oxen, out of the temple; and he poured out the coins of the money-changers and overturned their tables'.

The temple trade was a good business. It provided the people with a useful service. The prices were rather high, but the people could afford them. Yet Jesus saw through the excuses and recognized the idolatry.

The Jerusalem temple was meant to have been a place of sacrifice and prayer. It still was in Jesus' day, but the worship had been tainted by *mammon*.

The church today should also be characterized by a life of sacrifice and prayer. On the whole, it is – but we've also been polluted by the power of *mammon*. The love of money has stolen our compassion, stifled our worship and paralyzed our giving.

I believe that it's time for another cleansing. It's time for the church in North America, Western Europe and the world to be released from its bondage to *mammon* and to enter into the generosity of the all-giving God.

It's time for us to conquer our fears of not having enough, and to take hold of the giving hand of Jesus. He will gently guide us into the joyful delights of earthly generosity and towards the heavenly blessing of true riches.

Preparing to give

In this chapter I want to make some practical suggestions which should help us begin to translate our new biblical ideas into giving lives which are deeply pleasing to God.

Face up to our fears

The biggest problem for most of us is getting in touch with our feelings about money. We know what Jesus taught, but we still have deep fears and insecurities.

Many of us are threatened by Jesus' words. We're afraid that following him will leave us destitute, that we'll be 'ripped off' by dishonest people, that our families might suffer some hardships.

> We're afraid that following Jesus will leave us destitute and that we'll be 'ripped off' by dishonest people

We find it difficult to believe that we'll find joy in giving, that heavenly treasure is genuine, and that all our earthly needs will be supplied.

Some people are convinced that they have too little money. A few feel guilty that they have too much. Others are terrified that friends might over-estimate their wealth and think them greedy.

These sorts of fears often come from our childhood. If our parents were poor, we may find the thought of giving our possessions away terribly frightening. And if our parents were prosperous we may feel that frugality is a vice rather than a virtue.

It's important that we identify our fears about money. We should ask ourselves, 'What are we afraid of?' – and discuss the answers with our pastors. Then we can try to find out *why* we are fearful. Most people find that naming their fears is the first step on the road to defeating them.

Stop denying our wealth

Most North American and West European Christians have problems balancing their budgets. We tend to compare ourselves with our neighbors or employers, and often end up feeling poor in comparison.

It might help us if we started to examine ourselves in relation to all earth's humanity. We should face up to the undeniable fact that we are among the wealthiest people alive on this planet.

If we own a car or a home, we're in First Class. If we have fresh water on tap, electricity installed, and food in a cupboard, we belong to the planet's privileged few. In global terms, the mere fact that we can read this book means that we are extremely fortunate.

We shouldn't feel guilty about this. For some reason God has chosen to bless us greatly. But this blessing means that we have a special responsibility towards those who have less than we do.

Start acknowledging God's grace

Many of us are quick to announce that we have been saved *spiritually* by grace but some of us are slow to grasp that we still live *materially* by grace.

Nearly everyone reading this book is surrounded by signs of God's grace. God has given us a beautiful planet to enjoy, and most of us live in its more comfortable parts.

Our surroundings, our bodies, our families – all these are gifts from God. We have done nothing to deserve them and can do nothing to earn them.

God promised the children of Israel that he would give them 'great and goodly cities which you did not build, and houses full of all good things which you did not fill, and cisterns hewn out which you did not hew, and vineyards and olive trees which you did not plant' (Deuteronomy 6:10-11).

Isn't that our experience? Like the farmers of Israel, we can work hard and skillfully only to see our businesses affected by factors outside our control.

They could sow, weed and harvest, only for drought, fire, disease or war to destroy them.

Equally, many today have seen their incomes collapse because of recession, depression, interest rate rises, international trade wars, redundancy or accident. Just as much as a harvest of old, our personal

Just as much as a harvest of old, our income depends on the gracious provision of the all-giving God

incomes still depend on the gracious provision of the all-giving God.

We need to acknowledge these truths. We must confess with our mouths that we are not self-sufficient people, rather we live only by the grace of God. Surely our lives will be filled with joy, celebration and thanksgiving when we grasp the truth that our income is a grace-gift from God.

The general acceptance of this truth was one of the key reasons why most Jewish festivals centered on thanksgiving.

Talk about money honestly

If we're to be freed from the power of *mammon* to become cheerful givers like God, we need to be able to speak freely and honestly about our wealth and possessions.

Most people are more secretive about their incomes, and more sensitive about their assets, than anything else.

We are often convinced that people – even Christian friends – value us according to our wealth. We worry that they will look down on us if they learn we earn too little – or despise us if we earn too much.

> **Many people are more secretive about their income, more sensitive about their assets, than anything else**

We need Christian teaching which helps us relate to money more biblically. Many people spend so much time worrying about money – and think that they are the only ones who lose sleep in this way. It's not true, but they won't realize it until they hear others talk about their financial concerns.

Churches today need to foster an atmosphere of acceptance in which Christian people can confess their financial fears and temptations. We need small groups where people can find answers to their problems with money. And we need cheerfully to offer each other mutual support in the pilgrimage to generosity.

Many, many believers fail God over money. If we are to defeat *mammon*, we need churches where sinners can find financial forgiveness and healing.

This will only happen when we take the lid of this subject and start to talk about our reluctance to give; when we own up to our problem with trusting Jesus' words, and admit to our fears about acknowledging our wealth.

Know the poor

We've seen that God urges believers to give to the poor and needy. Yet many Christians today have lost touch with the poor. We tend to live in the more affluent neighborhoods and are often frightened to mix with the poor – who usually live in the dangerous parts of our towns.

When we can't see the poor, we form judgments about them which are based on media comment rather than first-hand knowledge. If we don't listen to the poor, we can't hear their pain. When we never eat with the poor, we live in a make-believe world which prevents us from 'loving our neighbors' in the way that Jesus intended. And if we refuse to worship with them, we deny the reality of Christ's united body in our town.

We can visit the poor, not to preach or patronize, but to learn from them. Some of us can live among them – as Jesus did. All of us can stop watching television programs which concentrate on the affluent and insulate us from the pain of the vast majority.

When we are traveling overseas, we can visit the homes of national pastors and missionaries to learn from them first-hand about life among the world's poorest people. Even better, we can spend a month volunteering for an aid or missionary agency.

Nothing changes the way that Western Christians give like a short spell living in the Third World!

Nothing changes the way that Western Christians give like a short spell actually living in the Third World!

But no matter how many books we read, videos we watch and missionaries we listen to, we'll only know the needs of the poor when we've eaten their food, walked with them to collect water, slept in their homes, cuddled their children and worshipped with them in their buildings.

Close contact with the poor is the best way that I know of loosening tight wallets! *Mammon* tries to keep us well away from the needy because he knows what God's love will do to our purses when we meet them.

Trust God

If we want to be blessed and cheerful givers, we have to trust God. Jesus encouraged his disciples to stop worrying and start trusting. His message is still the same today.

Too many believers allow money to make their decisions for them. 'Can we afford it?' they ask. But the question they should ask is, 'What does God want?' What happens when God suggests an action which we don't have enough money to carry out? Do we trust God? Or do we let money make our decision?

When God fed the Jews in the wilderness, they were allowed to collect enough manna only for that immediate day's needs.

> Do you allow money to make your decisions? Do you ask, 'Can I afford it?' or 'What does God want?'

In the Lord's Prayer, Jesus encourages us to ask God for food for just that day. Throughout the Bible, people are urged to meet the immediate needs of the poor. And we've seen Paul promise that God will supply his partners' needs.

Sadly, enough for today just isn't enough for too many modern believers. They want some spare for tomorrow as well. They might be able to trust God for the present, but they find it hard to trust him for next week as well.

But they don't have to, for we're not called to trust God today for tomorrow. Instead we're called to trust him today for today, *every* day. Christians are always worrying about the future – despite the fact that the Bible forbids this. It calls us to be different from pagans and to live one day at a time.

Generosity is easier when we realize that we don't need to

worry about tomorrow. It's helpful to cultivate the daily habit of asking ourselves whether God can provide for that day's needs. I guarantee our answer will always be 'Yes!'

We'll realize that trusting God to provide 'enough for today' is all the trust we need for our entire life

After a few months of this, people begin to realize that trusting God to provide 'enough for today' is all the trust they need for their lives. This discovery releases us from *mammon*'s hoarding spirit – which *always* quenches giving. We become free to experience the godly joy of generosity.

Recognize God's ownership

The Bible makes it clear that God owns everything. The whole world belongs to him. So God the Owner laid down clear financial rules for Israel which determined the way that they could use his land and treat his children.

The land had to lie fallow in every seventh year, and whatever came up then could be eaten only by the poor. In every fiftieth year, all slaves had to be set free, all debts canceled, and all land returned to its original owner.

The Jews obeyed these rules because they recognized that God was the ultimate owner of all things – he had the right to decide what happened to *his* property.

Our attitude to our possessions changes when we deeply acknowledge this truth. We won't become careless with things – who would dare to be casual with something which had been lent to us by Almighty God!

Instead, we will find it far easier to let go. We will thank God for lending one of his precious possessions to us for a short while, and will be glad that he is now lending it to someone else!

But most important of all, our acknowledgment of God's ownership will transform the way we think about giving.

Instead of wondering, 'How much of *my* money should I give to God?' we ask, 'How much of *God's* money should I keep for myself?'

When we catch ourselves asking this question, we can be sure that we are well on the way to becoming generous givers – ones who bring immense pleasure to God.

> Instead of thinking, 'How much of my money should I give to God?' we ask, 'How much of God's money should I keep for myself?'

Acknowledge our stewardship

Some people may be called to give all their money away as part of their conversion from *mammon* to Christ. But believers are not told – as a general rule – to give all their money away. Instead we are expected to steward it carefully on the real owner's behalf.

Jesus' parable of the talents, in Matthew 25, is clearly about finances. We're meant to make our money grow – not for ourselves, but as stewards for God and his kingdom. We are responsible for developing the possessions and wealth which God has entrusted to us. We can use them to make our own lives on earth more comfortable, or we can use them to earn ourselves heavenly treasure. It is up to us how we use our money. We decide. We are the stewards.

Some ministers encourage their members to delegate their decisions about giving to the leaders. They ask their members to direct *all* their giving to the local church and leave it to the leaders to decide how it is used.

But I don't think that we are meant to abdicate from our giving decisions. The early church gave gifts to the apostles only so that needy

> As stewards, we're called to make our money grow by hard work and careful investment

143

believers could be helped more effectively: they still personally gave their tithes, sacrifices and offerings when and how *they* chose.

As stewards, we are called to make our money grow by hard work and careful investment. Then we should manage our money following the biblical principles we've found.

We support – as partners – those ministries which God has used to bless us most. We start to repay our eternal debt to the Jews. We provide hospitality. We live in equality with our brothers and sisters overseas.

We give a tenth of our income to provide for local Christian leaders and the poor in our neighborhood. We help the needy. We give to express thanks to God. We control and direct our giving while we live, and also after our death through a generous will. And we do all this gladly and cheerfully, certain of a heavenly reward and confident that God will supply all our earthly needs.

We control and direct our giving while we live, and also after our death through a generous will

Principles of giving

There are four basic questions about Christian giving and receiving which need answers.

[1] Why should we give?

[2] How should we give?

[3] To whom should we give?

[4] What do we receive when we've given?

By now we should all be able to give biblical answers to each of these four questions. Please pause now and write a brief answer to each question on a separate piece of paper. We can check our answers as we read on further.

WHY SHOULD WE GIVE?

There seem to be seven main reasons why we should give our money, our wealth and our possessions away.

At various times, a different one of these reasons will be uppermost in our mind. But, over a period of time, they should all feature in our thinking and motivate our giving.

God gives

We've seen that God is introduced throughout the Bible as one who gives lavishly. Everything we know about God reveals him as the all-giving Creator and Redeemer.

God gives to all humanity – to his friends and enemies – without expecting anything in return. We want to be like him. We want to be more like Jesus. We want to think like him and act like him.

This means that we will give generously because we know that this is the God-like, Christ-like way to behave.

God commands us to give

We've read God's commands to the Jews in the Old Testament and have noted that he ordered them to make giving central in their personal, family and national lives.

We've examined Jesus' instructions to his disciples and have gazed at his encounters with different men and women. We've studied the rest of the New Testament teaching and now we should know for certain – beyond any shadow of doubt – that Almighty God commands us to give.

Now we know that we'll be disobeying God each time we fail to give when asked – and when we neglect to help a needy person

From now on, we know that we'll be disobeying God each time we fail to give when asked – and when we neglect to help a person whose needs we can see.

We love with God's love

We understand that 'God so loved the world that he gave', and are convinced that God gives because he loves – not for any self-seeking reason. We recognize that it's a natural human instinct to give to those we love, and we know that God expects us to love as he loves us – even our enemies.

Therefore we will give because we're filled with God's love – and because we know that our giving will help God's type of love to grow within us.

We're thankful

We've noticed that the Bible speaks repeatedly of thanks*giving*, rather than of thank*speaking*. We've seen that the Jews gave sacrificial gifts to God as one means of expressing their gratitude for the way he provided for all their needs. And now we recognize that we should begin to show our thanks to God by giving to him.

However – to have real meaning – this must be a special *extra* gift in thanks for something particular. Our regular weekly contribution at church can't be considered a special thanksgiving gift.

The Bible teaches that we give to God either by giving generously to a poor person or to a Christian ministry which has blessed us. So we should give a special love-gift to God in one of these ways whenever we want to thank him for a birth, or a job promotion, or for anything which means a great deal to us.

We want to create equality

We've seen how the believers' circle of giving responsibility gradually grew through the Bible. To begin with, Jewish people gave to help those nearest to them – to their families and needy people whom they could see and touch.

But by the end of the Scriptures, the first Christians had accepted that they had a duty to give to people whom they could not see – to traveling ministries, to believers in Israel, and to needy people far away overseas.

And we noted the New Testament teaches that this sort of giving creates equality among the brethren.

> The first Christians accepted that they had a duty to give to people whom they could not see – to traveling ministries, believers in Israel, and needy people overseas

Today, we're all aware of the massive variations in wealth around the world. We know that some of our brothers and sisters in the Third World struggle to survive in appalling conditions while we live in relative ease and luxury. So we give to them in an attempt to create some sort of equality between us, and because we recognize the essential unity of Christ's body.

We know John taught that we can't have God's love within us if we ignore our brothers' needs. This means that we'll give with generosity because we can't do nothing while some of our Third World sisters sleep by the roadside.

We want heavenly treasure

We've read all about God's wonderful promises of divine blessing, great rewards, heavenly treasure – even the inheritance of a kingdom. So we'll give because we want to earn as much heavenly treasure as we can.

We hope to be among those favored believers who receive

the awesome blessing which God has promised for those who give generously in the way he prescribes.

We long for that treasure. We know that it's infinitely preferable to anything available on earth. We're certain that it is worth any amount of sacrifice. So we'll

> We give because we want to receive the best possible reward from the all-giving God

give because we want to receive the best possible heavenly reward and commendation from the all-giving God.

We want our needs supplied

We've read God's awesome promises which guarantee that all our needs will be met when we give in God's way.

Many people spend years clinging on to their money in a vain attempt to meet their own needs, only to see God provide miraculously as soon as they start to give. Sadly, many never learn to give and stay in need to the end.

Some of us have serious needs in our lives. But none of us have needs which are too great for the all-giving God!

No matter whether we have enormous debts or very poor health. Regardless of all the difficulties in our homes and families. God promises to supply *all* our needs out of his infinite riches *when* we give in his way.

So we will have no shame in giving to have our needs met. We tithe for our leaders' salaries. We give to the Jews and a ministry partner. We provide hospitality for strangers and

> None of us have needs which are too great for the all-giving God!

care for the poor. And we do all this because we know that our generous God will honor our sacrificial giving by supplying every need that we have.

How should we give?

Some people today view their giving rather like their taxes. It is all duty and no joy. They get it out of the way by sending a cheque for a certain percentage of their income to their local church or to some charitable organization.

They've eased their conscience, and the church allocates the donation. But this isn't the best way to give. We'll never find deep joy this way. Based on the biblical principles we've examined, here are five suggestions for a giving pattern which is relevant to modern society.

Give generously

We now know that we are called by God to be generous. We can't avoid this basic truth. But there are many different ways open to us of showing our generosity.

For example, we're not really generous if we place an extra 10% in the Sunday collection but ignore beggars in the street and bin letters from charities. And we are not biblically generous if we persist in measuring our giving by what we donate rather than by what we retain.

Generosity means giving widely rather than restricting our giving to one or two favored causes. It means giving to all the different types of people and projects we've considered, for all the different reasons we've seen.

God's giving is generous because it embraces friends and enemies, it encompasses all humanity. We should follow him by ensuring that we give widely in *his* way.

Give appropriately

Because we are stewards of God's money, we should give in the way that *he* wants. This means that supporting people in ministry will be the focus of our giving.

Throughout the Bible, we've seen that giving is essentially to meet the needs of *people*. So we'll do well to check that

> **We should give in the way that God wants. This means supporting people in ministry will be the focus of our giving**

most of our giving goes to supporting people – especially people in ministry.

When we give to an organization – no matter whether a church, a television ministry or overseas mission – we should follow the Old Testament freewill-offering principle.

The Jews knew exactly what was needed, what their gifts would be used for, and how much was required. Their giving was carefully targeted to meet clearly defined needs.

For example, in our ministry we try to be as specific as possible. Our monthly donor-letter ministry always directs our partners and friends to precise needs in our evangelistic missions, in our training of nationals to reach their nations for Christ, in our worldwide Jewish outreach, and so on. They always know exactly what the free-will gifts they send will accomplish.

I think that we would do well to ensure that we give to reputable organizations which always explain what they need our gifts for – and which always report back so we know that our gifts have been used properly.

Give personally

During the last few years, most modern giving has become very impersonal. We usually give by bank transfers or a

> **Face-to-face giving stretches our generosity and greatly increases our joy**

cheque through the mail. It's hard to find joy in this sort of impersonal giving when we don't actually hand over our gifts in person or see the individual we're helping.

Face-to-face giving stretches our generosity and greatly increases our joy. Obviously it's not always feasible to give in cash and in person. But we can ensure that at least some aspects of our giving are made in person – for example, at crusades, seminars and meetings.

A few of us could make an annual visit to the local office of a ministry or charity we support to hand over our gift in small denomination notes. This would be much more meaningful to us than impersonal bank transfers.

Give creatively

We've seen that God gives in a wide variety of ways, and have noted that Old and New Testament giving was broad and varied. It included tithes, sacrifices, free-will offerings, gleanings, hospitality, funds for widows, collections for famine relief, expensive jars of oil – even a new tomb.

Somehow we need to recapture both the ceremony and the enormous variety of biblical giving. For the Jews, worship was giving, and gifts were a major part of all their religious ceremonies and celebrations. Far too often today 'the collection' is an embarrassed ritual hidden in a brisk hymn.

We will only restore giving to its rightful place by making much more time for offerings in our services. We must find more creative ways for people to give than merely putting coins in a bag to be spent on heating bills by the Treasurer.

We will only restore giving to its rightful place by making much more time for offerings in our services

We can use offerings to inform people about needs and to teach about rewards. We can invite the homeless to special meals, hold promise auctions for Third World projects, and give our gifts in small coins so that we get back in touch with our giving.

We must develop creative ways of making *people* central

to our giving – so that our tithes really do release many more families into ministry.

Give thoughtfully

While we should aim to be believers who are characterized by God's cheerful generosity, we don't want to be people who give casually or thoughtlessly.

We do want to give at every opportunity and to all who ask. But we don't want to give without thinking about what we are doing.

We should ask ourselves, 'Why am I giving?' or 'Why am I not giving?' We can check our reasons and learn whether they match with biblical principles.

We can take pains to discover how much a person or organization needs – and establish whether our gift is too much, too little or just right for that need.

We can learn whether it would be more helpful to give a small amount regularly or a large sum occasionally. And – of course – we should always know how much of God's money we are keeping back for ourselves.

These questions are not to make us introspective. Rather they are to help us become responsible givers who recognize that Western Christians have an enormous financial responsibility for the body of Christ around the world.

TO WHOM SHOULD WE GIVE?

This is probably the most important question for nearly all modern believers. We see massive needs in our cities and on our television screens. We hear frequent financial appeals in our churches and receive regular letters from large numbers of ministries and charities. We often feel swamped by the demands placed on our giving. Which ones should we respond to? Whom should we ignore?

It's too easy to opt out from the struggle by giving to only one cause, or a token amount to every society that's purchased our address on a mailing list. However, the Bible contains giving principles

> We often feel swamped by the demands placed on our giving. Which ones should we respond to? Whom should we ignore?

which can help us through the maze of requests into the place of cheerful, generous joy.

Here are seven principles which I've distilled from the different material we've examined in the Scriptures.

Give to local 'priests and levites'

The first priority in our giving should be to allocate a tenth of our income to supporting people in our own locality.

Local churches often encourage their members to give 'tithes and offerings'. This biblical principle means that the first tenth of family income goes to the church – plus a generous amount above that. In my opinion, the offerings should be used to cover the overhead expenses of the church, while the tithes should be used *only* to support people.

Somehow we need to do our best to ensure that the bulk of our tithes are used to finance the modern equivalents of priests and levites. That's all those people who are involved in some form of full or part-time Christian work – secretaries, musicians, youth workers, counselors, caretakers, pastors, missionaries and so on.

> Too many churches use members' tithes to pay electricity bills rather than using them only to support people

Most churches have sent a missionary overseas: these can be fully supported through tithes. Instead of being spent mostly on themselves, two-thirds of the members' tithes from a church with a hundred members would easily support four families. If our churches would only return to

153

the biblical 'tithes for people' principle we could release a massive number of people into the work of the gospel.

Give to local needy

One of the great works of the Holy Spirit in recent years has been teaching evangelical, pentecostal and charismatic churches that good works should go alongside the proclamation of the gospel. These works are beginning to complement our preaching.

More and more churches are starting orphanages, taking clothes and food to the homeless, organizing play-groups for single parents, running drop-in centers for the unemployed, and delivering meals to the elderly. They are doing this as an expression of God's love which speaks as loudly as the gospel they preach.

In this ministry, we have poured financial resources into an orphanage just across the border in Mexico. At some of our North American missions, we now provide workers, clothes and food for the homeless – as well as special transport to our meetings. And, when we are overseas, we always do our best to feed the vast crowds who come for training.

An awesome work of caring for the destitute could be carried out by churches if tithes were used in this scriptural way

In the Old Testament, one third of the people's tithes provided food stores which were used to feed the needy in that area. A similar proportion of our tithes could go into a fund today which churches used to help their local poor.

If churches kept their members' tithes separate from other funds, it would be easy to ensure that tithes were used in this biblical way – exclusively for people.

Just think of the good that one third of the members'

tithes could accomplish in our neighborhoods! An awesome work of caring for the destitute could be carried out by churches if our tithes were used in this scriptural way.

Give to God's ministry for you

After our tithe, our second priority should be to support – with committed, regular sacrificial gifts – the ministry which God has used to bless us the most.

We noted in the New Testament that Macedonian believers were committed, long term partners of Paul. They couldn't travel with him; but they could pray for him, and they could give to support his work. We saw that Paul considered their

If we've been brought to faith by one of these ministers – or blessed through their tapes and books – we should stand with them as a committed partner

gifts to be on a par with Old Testament sacrifices which were offered directly to God.

These givers were people who had been brought to faith in Christ by Paul. As well as supporting their local church leaders, they also supported his traveling ministry *and* his special appeals for funds for work among the Jews.

That same pattern continues today. Most teachers are called to local ministry. But a few are sent out by God in traveling ministries across the world.

If we've been brought to faith by one of these ministers – or blessed through their tapes and books – we should consider standing with them as committed partners.

I depend on my partners. Without their prayers and giving I would not be able to preach to vast crowds in distant lands. Without their sacrificial donations, I would not have been able to train hundreds of thousands of national leaders around the world. Without their constant support and encouragement, I would despair at the enormity of the task which God has given me.

Give hospitality to visitors

We've seen the vital place of hospitality right through the Bible. We've noted that we're charged with a special responsibility of giving hospitality to God's servants. We've read all the New Testament orders to make hospitality a priority. We remember that whenever we welcome a visitor we're actually welcoming God. And we've been gripped by Jesus' pleas to invite social outcasts into our homes.

More than any other aspect of our giving, hospitality involves our time, our love, our homes and ourselves. We can send money through the post to anyone, but we have to provide hospitality in person.

It's one thing to toss some money into a homeless person's bowl, but quite another matter to invite them into our homes. Yet surely this is what we are called to do – and what will draw them to Christ.

As our communities disintegrate, families break up, and the number of elderly people multiplies, hospitality becomes ever more urgent. Our towns are increasingly filled with lonely people who'd value a meal in another's home.

> As our communities disintegrate, families break up, and the number of elderly people multiplies, hospitality becomes more urgent

Many elderly believers live alone, long distances from their families. Yet most of them have empty rooms that they could use for the kingdom – but only if they can break free from *mammon's* protective spirit towards property.

Over a third of the people in most Western churches are now single – it's a crazy waste of kingdom resources for them to live and eat alone all the time. Hospitality needs to be taught, encouraged, modeled and demonstrated in every church in our land.

Give to the poor

All believers have a general duty to be generous to the poor. We should consider that the wealth we're stewarding for God is always available to them. But we're not called to give everything to the needy as our main financial priority.

As well as the lesser part of their tithe, Old Testament Jews also had to treat the poor fairly and provide for them creatively through practices like gleaning. In the New Testament, we saw that Jesus treated the poor with respect and encouraged his disciples to give generously to them.

Our attitude to immigrants, ethnic minorities and social outcasts is a key test of our love

Our attitude to ethnic minorities, immigrants and social outcasts is a key test of our love. Do we respect them? Do we value and welcome them? Or do we look down on them and think of them as inferior?

Many churches have lost touch with the poor. Somehow we need to re-integrate ourselves with them – especially with immigrant groups. As we mix with them, we'll naturally give to them in creative and practical ways.

We also have a duty towards the poor in the Third World. We know something of their desperate needs from the media and missionaries.

Like the early church, we can only give to them through an organized fund. There has to be trust in this. The first believers trusted Paul to pass on the money they gave, and they trusted the poor to spend it wisely. But they didn't issue a list of instructions – their giving wasn't conditional.

We should give to organizations we trust. Groups with Spirit-filled people responsible for the finances. Ministries which don't impose their will on the poor, but empower them instead. The poor in the Third World may need our financial giving, but they don't need our financial control.

All our giving should liberate, not enslave; equip, not control; build up, not bind or humiliate.

Give to the Jews

Paul made it plain that we have an eternal spiritual debt to the Jews. Where would we be without them?

Sometimes we forget that Jesus was a Jew, that all the first Christians were Jews, and that almost all of the Bible was written by Jews.

Giving to Jews and to Christian work in Israel should be very high on our list of giving priorities

Jewish believers brought the Gospel to Gentiles, and first spread the Good News across the world. Yet instead of expressing gratitude, for centuries the church persecuted the Jews or turned a blind eye when others persecuted them.

It's time to listen to Paul and start repaying our debt. I strongly believe that giving to Jews and to work in Israel should be on our list of giving priorities.

Give to God

I'm sure that there isn't one of us who doesn't long to give to God. Even before we started reading this book, we knew that we wouldn't hold anything back from him.

Now we know how we can give to him – directly and personally! We've read Jesus' words and have finally understood that giving to a needy person is giving to God.

And we've grasped Paul's teaching that sacrificial giving

to an anointed ministry is personally offering God a sacrifice which brings him great pleasure!

We must never forget these simple truths, or let anyone make us doubt them, or be tricked into *adding* to them. Remember, God is personal, so we give to him by giving to a person – either by helping somebody in need or supporting someone in a ministry or a church.

Whenever we want to express thansk*giving* to God we should give to him in one of the ways described in the Scriptures.

WHAT DO WE RECEIVE FROM OUR GIVING?

Some teachers do not think that this is a question we should ever ask. Yet it is a question which the Bible keeps on answering. We've seen that many clear promises are made – but only to those who give consistently in the way that God prescribes.

Heavenly treasure

Imagine that Britain decided to change its entire currency to US dollars, and that when it did all pounds would be worthless. Suppose also that nobody knew when this monetary conversion would take place.

Surely wise British families would turn most of their pounds into American dollars – keeping back just enough pounds to live on day to day.

That's the biblical picture. We can't take our wealth with us when we die, and we don't know when that will be. But we can turn our income and assets into something far more valuable – into eternal riches.

We convert our earthly wealth into heavenly treasure by giving it in God's way – by investing it in people.

Please don't forget all the *eternal* blessings we've read about – the heavenly treasure and eternal kingdom which the New Testament promises for those believers who give in God's way.

Read again these glorious passages and underline both the promises *and* the conditions: Matthew 10:40-42; Matthew 25:31-40; Luke 6:30-38; Luke 12:33-34; Luke 14:12-14; 2 Corinthians 9:6-14; Philippians 4:15-20.

> We convert our earthly wealth into heavenly treasure by giving it in God's way – by investing it in people

As you read these verses, note how the promises of *heavenly* blessings are for those who give to people – to the poor, to the Jews, and to men and women in Christian ministry to the church. Heavenly treasure and an eternal kingdom are our rewards where we give in faith to these groups of people.

Earthly needs

Some believers worry that their giving will make them worse off. They have no need to worry, for the Bible makes it plain that God will supply *all* our needs. But, remember, he decides what our needs are, not us!

Mammon will try to deceive us into thinking that giving will impoverish us. But in Philippians 4:19, Paul promises those who have given that 'My God shall supply all your needs according to his riches in glory by Christ Jesus'. And in Matthew 6:19-33, Jesus promises that God will provide us with everything we need when we put his *mammon*-rejecting kingdom first in our lives.

We have to decide whether we believe the Bible or *mammon*. But we can't obey both of them!

In this book, we've seen that both the Old and New Testament contain clear promises that God will bless us on earth in a tangible way which changes our earthly resources.

Please remember the special promises we've read for

following God's tithing principles. In Deuteronomy 14:29, he promises to bless the work of those who tithe in his way. And in Malachi 3:10, God promises overflowing blessing for those who tithe biblically.

These promises must mean that we can expect God to *more* than meet our earthly needs when we tithe properly. If we are employers, we can expect our business to prosper; and if we are employees, we can expect security and advancement.

Deuteronomy 24:19 contains a similar special promise. When we give freely to the poor we can expect God to bless whatever we do. This isn't spiritual blessing reserved for heaven, it is a clear promise that our work will prosper when we give in God's way.

> *Mammon* says that giving will impoverish us. Jesus promises that God will provide all our needs. We decide whom we believe

Isaiah 58:7-11 promise that we will receive incredible blessings when we give like God. He promises us health, guidance and good things – when we provide generous hospitality to both the homeless and the poor.

And we'll never forget the promises Paul made to those who gave to the Jews. Every single one of our needs will be met – our debts, family and employment problems, health, and so on. God personally guarantees to meet all our earthly needs when we give cheerfully and generously to his chosen people.

Growth and miracles

The book of Acts has shown us that God blesses givers in quite unexpected ways. The staggering church growth of the first Christians is clearly related to their generosity. The miracles of healing and deliverance shouldn't be separated from the sacrificial lifestyle of the disciples.

When our churches give in God's way we can expect to be blessed in equally wonderful ways. We can expect the gift of miracles. We can anticipate dynamic growth. We can look for stunning provision. God loves cheerful givers – and he delights to bless them in the biblical ways we have seen.

Giving takes faith. And we have a trustworthy God who is not going to ask us to do something which will harm us. He is the all-giving God, and we have learnt from the scriptures that he's asking us to follow him along the pathway of generosity.

I trust that we'll join together in the great adventure of giving like God. When we do, I know that we'll become cheerful and greatly blessed believers – who will receive God's great rewards both in this life and the life to come.

GIVERS TODAY

Until now, this book has been mainly theory. I've tried to show what the Bible teaches about giving so that we can start to think about giving in God's way.

But I'm sure that some readers want to know whether the theory actually works in practice today. There are always people who worry whether God can do in the present what he did in the past for the early church.

So, in this final chapter, I'm going to introduce a few of my partners. These are the men and women from a wide variety of denominational and ethnic backgrounds who have been helped by this ministry. They pray for the work that I do, and they give to finance the work of the gospel around the world – but especially in Israel.

As we read their stories, we can see how God has supplied all their needs as they've given sacrificially to this work.

Some have been healed, others have been released from the bondage of debt, a few have started work. Many of them gave generously when they themselves were in desperate financial need. We know now that God blesses exactly this sort of sacrificial giving. Some of them gave specifically to Israel, and – again – I hope that we now expect this sort of giving to be blessed by God.

As we read their stories, we shouldn't concentrate on the sums they contributed. Remember, God measures what we keep back, not what we give. Instead, we should look at their circumstances and see how God changes them.

Make ready to see the principles we've unearthed working in real-life situations. Prepare to praise God for his grace and goodness. Never forget, he does keep his promises.

Mary Montgomery

"In March 1993, I had been without work for over two years. The only income I had was $36 (£22) every two weeks. I was $4,000 (£2,500) behind with my rent.

Although I needed to keep the money, I gave $30 (£19) to MCWE's Jewish Outreach. Then the enemy spoke to me and asked me why I was sending money to reach Jews when I had my own problems right here in the South Bronx of New York. He told me that I was crazy. But I knew that the Jews were God's chosen people, and if God wanted me to give to them – and would bless me – I would do it.

> I surrendered everything to God and – in one month – a charity agency paid my entire back rent

I surrendered everything to God and – in one month – a charity agency paid my entire back rent. I had struggled so much in my own strength, but God did it quickly and without a struggle.

Later God opened up jobs for me which provided financial blessings in my life. Eventually, he gave me the job that I really wanted in a hospital.

This is amazing for someone like me who was a drug addict for twenty years. I sold drugs and ran a 'crack house'. God has changed my life and done so much for me."

Denise Murray

"I was a pastor's wife for fifteen years. Because of church pressures, our marriage was breaking up. I wanted out of everything. I even wanted a divorce. My husband and I had no jobs. There was nobody that I could trust.

I knew Morris Cerullo's ministry would help me. I went to his 1991 meeting in Chicago expecting total deliverance. At the service, I rededicated my life to God. During the offering, I gave $100 (£62) for me and $100 for my husband.

> Two days after the meeting, my husband got the highest paying job in the district as a manager in a grocery chain

Two days after the meeting, my husband got the highest paying job in the district as a manager in a grocery chain – and I received a job at the Marriott Hotel. That same week, my son quit taking drugs.

I also attended Morris Cerullo's 1994 meeting in Chicago. During the offering, he asked us to give $100 to the Jews! We did, but my husband and I needed help. Due to a recent accident, we were $10,000 (£6,250) in debt. When I went home, I went directly to the mailbox and found a cheque for exactly $10,000. This was money we had been trying to get from his company because of the accident."

Benny Smith

"I was watching the Victory television program in March 1993 when I heard Morris Cerullo prophesy that people who contributed to the work of the Lord would experience God's miracle of debt cancellation.

I believed what I heard and felt that I should give $100. I gave this and waited for the miracle of debt-cancellation.

At that point in my life, I was preparing to file for personal bankruptcy. I was $100,000 (£62,500) in debt and was deeply concerned about my wife and our four children. It appeared that I was going to lose everything, including my home. The situation looked hopeless. My job would never provide enough money to pay back all the debts that my family had as a result of sickness.

My job would never provide enough money to pay back all the debts

It began happening fast! The electric company called to say that the $1,100 (£687) owed to them was canceled! They even told me they would re-establish my credit!

Then, I received the news that $6,000 (£3,750) had been cut off my car loan and I no longer owed that money! Five other bills totaling $5,000 (£3,125) were also canceled.

Finally, my lawyer called me and told me that 'somehow' it had been determined that I could keep my home."

Mr & Mrs Donald Wilsie

"We first met Dr Cerullo nearly thirty years ago in Casper, Wyoming, where we pastored a church before Donald was injured in a car wreck and disabled.

Morris asked us to give $300 (£187) and Donald pledged to do this. In the following months and years we lost contact with the ministry of Dr Cerullo and for thirty years we did not fulfil that pledge. Two months before the Chicago Partners' Seminar, in 1992, some dear friends sent us information about Dr Cerullo.

Our financial situation was terrible. We had no money, but God provided finances for us to go to the seminar – and we took with us $300 finally to fulfil our pledge. We were giving all we had.

Incredibly, our small business began to grow rapidly. We had been at a $0 balance, but in seven weeks we showed a $200,000 (£125,000) balance.

Donald was also healed of diabetes. He had been taking medication for years, but was able to quit the medication. Donald knew that God had healed him.

Three months after the Chicago meeting, we put $17,000 (£10,625) in the offering. We had gone from barely being able to give a twenty-eight year old $300 pledge to being able to contribute $17,000.

We have a small business that is doing overwhelmingly well! When we went to Chicago, I began this business with one computer and printer. I now have ten computers and printers and am spread from Canada to the Gulf of Mexico.

We have been faithful in giving to Morris Cerullo's ministry. God has blessed us with both a brand new van and a truck. We also bought a new home – even though the offer we made to the buyers was ridiculous."

> Three months after the Chicago meeting, we put $17,000 in the offering

Juan Arevalo

"During the forty days of fasting and prayer initiated by MCWE in 1994, I received the 'Step One' letter from Morris Cerullo. God put on my heart to give $80 (£50) in the offering. I did not know where I would get the money, but I took a step in faith.

It was not easy to pay the pledge I had made. I had some obstacles. I had to obey God and put the problems aside! Two days after I sent the money, I received a letter from my employer saying that I was going to get a pay increase retroactive to 1991! Glory to God!

Our wages were supposed to be frozen until 1996 because of the Social Contract Act for government employees, but Pay Equity Management Board was giving raises only to people in my classification.

My retroactive cheque was $1,638.18! (£1,023). I can't stop praising God. He is so good to us! He supplies all our needs according to his riches in glory by Christ Jesus!"

Raejeanne Mueller

"I became a Christian in 1977. For about ten years I fed on the Bible. I began to get a taste of what it was like to put God's word to work in my life and to see the results – to understand what it is to walk in the Spirit.

In 1987, my husband's health was taken so that he could no longer work at all. We lost our trucking business. Within two weeks we had zero income. Under these circumstances, I was put into a position where I could do nothing in my own strength or power. I had to trust in God to be my provider.

God faithfully and miraculously provided for us. I was active in church during this time. However, after a church split and a very difficult time in relationships, I stopped going to church.

During the next four years I isolated myself in my home. It felt like God had abandoned me. I stopped hearing his voice. I began to listen to the lies and condemning thoughts of the enemy. I felt like I was losing my mind. I was filled with confusion and depression. I couldn't concentrate on anything or remember things. I paced around my house like a caged animal. I couldn't sleep at night. I was always physically weak and tired. I knew something was wrong but felt powerless to pray. I could not concentrate or comprehend when I tried to read God's Word.

> We lost our trucking business. Within two weeks we had zero income. We had to trust in God to be our provider

My daughter told me about MCWE's fast in 1993. She

was so excited about taking part that I decided to join her. Together we fasted one meal a day for twenty-one days.

Towards the end of the fast, Morris Cerullo wrote asking us to give something that was valuable to us to his ministry.

I prayed and asked God what he wanted me to give. He said, 'The $1,000 (£625) you pledged in 1992 but never gave'. God had to deal with my heart before I would give this. My

> God had to deal with my heart before I would give this amount. It had become hardened

heart had become hardened. I wasn't going to give it. God is more concerned about our hearts and why we give, and how we give than in our giving.

At the end of the fast I cheerfully gave the $1,000 to God through this ministry. My mind started clearing. The pressure in my head left and I could sleep at night. I started to hear from God again. I began to read and understand his word once more!

However, in 1988, a lien or charge for $50,000 (£31,250) had been put against our house by the State of California's Department of Industrial Relations. A friend had come into partnership with my husband to start a trucking business. He injured his back and claimed he was an employee and not a partner – he wanted compensation. When we went to court, we lost the case.

With interest, this lien had risen to $90,000 by the beginning of 1994. It could rise again. I wrote a letter to the State of California explaining to them exactly what had happened in this case. But they would not listen.

In January 1994, I made another $1,000 pledge to the Jewish World Outreach. When I heard about MCWE's forty day fast, I decided to participate and wrote to Morris Cerullo asking him to pray for us to receive a debt cancellation of the lien.

I also wrote another letter to the State of California, explaining a second time what had happened in the case against us. This letter was identical to the first letter which had been declined.

On April 6th, I sent my cheque for $1,000 to MCWE to pay my pledge. On April 11th, I received a Notice of Debt Cancellation of the lien totaling $90,277.84.

I give God the glory for all the good things he has done for me and my family. I believe this is all due to the change of my heart in giving cheerfully. My husband who had been disabled since 1986 has also recently returned to work."

Marvin & Margie Rudolph

"In 1977, Morris Cerullo came to Birmingham, Alabama, and ministered in the Parliament House Hotel.

At that time, we ran a little newspaper called 'The Jewish Star'. (We are 'completed' Jews.) But the paper was about to go under. We wanted God to prosper it and had been asking him to save our business. We decided to ask Morris Cerullo to pray with us for it. He put the newspaper under his arm and carried it to his hotel room.

God answered this prayer seventeen years ago, and today we have a strong newspaper business which has taken us around the world twice. We have met two Prime Ministers of Israel, as well as President Reagan, President Bush and a host of other important leaders."

John Bell

"Because of what happened to me in Vietnam, I had a sickness called Post Traumatic Stress Disorder. I was in

Vietnam from July 1968 to July 1969. It was some of the hardest times of my life.

When I came out of Vietnam, I had no money and no benefits. I was destitute, homeless, on the street. I couldn't hold down a job.

I had been a drug addict and alcoholic for years. Although I was born again in 1978, I was still taking drugs.

> I had no money and no benefits. I was destitute, homeless, on the street

I began taking drugs when I went to Vietnam. I got into smoking marijuana, then harder stuff like heroin and opium. When I came out of the service I started taking cocaine.

I tried really hard to stop, but circumstances would happen in my life and I would go back to drugs. I was walking around being defeated, like most Christians. I kept crying out to God, 'When is my life going to change?' Then it started.

In 1990 I was walking down the street in San Jose, California. I was depressed and discouraged because I was having trouble on my job and was going through a divorce.

Suddenly, I saw a piece of colorful paper on the ground. I picked it up and found that it was a brochure telling about a crusade with Morris Cerullo.

My life was transformed at the 1990 San Jose Crusade. I was totally set free from all drugs and alcohol. God gave me a purpose for living and filled me with joy and peace like I'd never known. My life was changed when I became a partner with Morris Cerullo.

Two years later, I went to one of Dr Cerullo's meetings in San Jose. During the service, he looked out at me in the audience and said, 'Watch that man in the green shirt'.

Then he asked me if I was ready. I started to tremble. I nodded my head. He put out his hand and said, 'Take it.' Rivers of God's love hit me like a freight train. I lay praying

171

in tongues and was just lost in love. It was like God came down and put his arms around me.

I felt God moving through me! Suddenly my ear popped. Ten years earlier I had lost all but 20% of my hearing after an accident. The doctor said nothing could be done. But that night in San Jose, God touched me and I could hear perfectly. I went back to the doctor and he said that I had what looked like a brand new eardrum with no hole.

From 1990 to 1994, God has brought me from nothing to 100% income. In 1990, I was in a VA program. I was homeless. I didn't have anything. I got 10% from my VA pension which is only $86 (£54) a month. On top of that I received only $30 (£19) from social security.

In 1992 at the San Jose crusade, Morris Cerullo gave a prophecy. He said, 'If you will dig down and plant a seed into this ministry, God will give it back'. I didn't have any money. So I went around and begged for money. I think I raised $40. Instead of putting it in my pocket because I didn't have any food or anything at that time, I said, 'Father, I am going to give this to you'. I put it in the offering. God richly blessed me.

From 1990 to 1994, God has brought me from nothing to 100% income

Right after that, my VA pension went from 10% to 50%. My VA income increased from $86 to $550. I also began to receive full benefits from SSD – plus $9,000 (£5,625) in back benefits. On top of this I was given a cheque from the VA for $15,000 back benefits. My income had increased to over $1,000 (£625) a month.

Every time I would get a lump of income, I would plant a seed into the Kingdom of God. God has made me a cheerful giver. God said, 'If you will step out in faith and support Dr Cerullo's ministry, I will bless you mightily'.

At the beginning of 1994, I pledged $1,000 to Operation

Israel. This was a step of faith, because I had only $48 (£30) in my pocket. I emptied out my bank account to give. Six months later, I received a 100% increase in my VA pension. My monthly VA income rose to $1,849 a month for life. With the SSD, I get a total of $2,833 month for life. God has supplied my needs."

> God has made me a cheerful giver. God said, 'If you will step out in faith and support Dr Cerullo's ministry, I will bless you back mightily'

Dr Tresiaty Pohe

Tresiaty leads a clinic in Jakarta, Indonesia. She attended MCWE's 1993 World Conference with only $100 in her pocket. At that time money was not coming into her clinic. She had no money in the bank and a $7,000 debt.

At the 1993 Conference, Tresiaty pledged $15,000 (£9,325) to the Jewish World Outreach. When she returned to Indonesia, Tresiaty prayed, 'God, give me money so that I can pay my pledge'. It was due on March 1st.

During the last week of February, Tresiaty was unexpectedly given $25,000. She was able to pay her pledge and repay her debt.

Then her clinic income for March rose to $85,000. People were fighting to get into the clinic. There were not enough rooms for all the people. Many of them became Christians. And Tresiaty was given $50,000 to install exercise equipment in the clinic.

Dale Pfeil

"I went to Morris Cerullo's Chicago Partners' Seminar in 1992. I gave about $1,500 (£938) in offerings, paid for three other people to go to the seminar and also gave my meal tickets away. The only money that I had left was for fuel to drive home.

I also attended MCWE's 1993 World Conference. I gave about $1,500 in offerings even though I was in financial trouble. I took seven people with me to that conference and paid for everything.

> God has called me to take evangelists to places where they can receive good teaching

God has called me to take evangelists – and people who want to serve God fully – to places where they can receive good teaching and become spiritually stronger.

A man that I met at the Chicago Seminar was also at the World Conference. He gave me $56,000 (£35,000) to use in our ministry. After the conference my business started to prosper. That month we did $12,000 worth of business; the next, $26,000; the month after, $51,000; then $63,000 and $73,000. As a result I was able to clear my $70,000 debt.

I am in the masonry business. I do stone work. Six months after the World Conference, I did a job for a big company in Charlotte. I needed about $8,000 worth of boulders and $8,000 worth of top soil. God gave me both the boulders and the top soil for nothing.

I take evangelists all round the country to preach the gospel. I believe in supporting people who are wise with God's money.

I've learnt to 'cast my bread out on the water'. It hasn't always came back the way I expected – it's not like planting tomatoes. Many times, the harvest has arrived ten years after the planting."

Mr & Mrs Jerome Rhames

"We attended Morris Cerullo's 21st World Conference when he encouraged everyone to give $100 in the offering for financial deliverance in their own personal lives.

We had come to that conference on our last dollar. I had brought an offering to give. But my wife felt that she should give another $100 by faith, so she filled out an offering card. We saw no means of getting the money, but believed God when Morris Cerullo asked everyone to give.

We'd been fighting a legal battle for a long time. We had been told that we wouldn't get anything, but after the Conference we were surprised to receive a cheque in the mail for over $800. So we immediately sent our pledge to MCWE.

I also received a letter at the beginning of 1992 from MCWE inviting us to become elders. We did not have the money for the plane trip to fly to San Diego for the special Elders' meeting. But we prayed and told God that if this was his will, we would look to him to provide the money. Unexpectedly we received a cheque in the mail for $5,000 as compensation for a job-related accident I'd had. It was ten times what we were looking to receive! This money came just in time for us to go to San Diego. We are walking in total provision, continual supply. Praise God."

> We saw no means of getting the money, but believed God when Morris Cerullo asked everyone to give

Mr & Mrs Ed Gavin

"We've been partners with Morris Cerullo for over ten years. During this time, many of our prayers have been answered. We have six children and have been married for thirty four years.

In the past, work has been scarce for my husband, Ed. He has been in construction for the past twenty-five years. One year he made only $5,000 (£3,125).

When we heard about tithing, we did the best we could

and in 1984 Dr Cerullo sent a letter to say that he was agreeing in prayer for our financial situation. He prophesied that my husband's income would double the following year.

Well, Ed's income did not double. It tripled!

We were able to buy our own home in New York. The God we serve is a God of provision for every need we have. We are now financially secure. Ed holds a good job and God has provided well.

Recently, we had another financial blessing which came unexpectedly. I enjoy working and taking care of retarded Hasidic Jewish children. Several years ago I fell and hurt my right leg. Some friends told me I should sue the organization, but I didn't feel right about that. However, God worked it all for good. Just a few months ago, Worker's Compensation called and said they would give me $7,000 (£4,375) for the time that I could not work as a result of the injury! God just keeps giving and giving!"

> **When we heard about tithing, we did the best we could**

Mr & Mrs Emmanuel Kurkjian

"I am the manager of an auto repair shop at a Shell Gas Station. In 1992 I was $75,000 (£46,875) in debt. This included $25,000 (£15,625) that I owed my brother for my home. The property was in his name. I was only making $1,000 (£626) a week and was barely making ends meet.

I couldn't afford to give $1,000 to a ministry. I didn't think I could ever do that. Yet I did at the Chicago Partners' Seminar in 1992.

God spoke to me that I was to give $1000. I said, 'Dr Cerullo is my partner. I am going to give.' I made up my mind to give. I surrendered my business to God. At this stage I wasn't giving my tithe or offering. But I started at the conference and my financial picture changed.

All of a sudden, people started coming in to my business. I found myself making three times more than in the previous year – $3,000 (£1,875) a week.

> I wasn't giving my tithe or offering. But I started at the conference and my financial picture changed

I never thought my home would be under my name, but I was able to pay off $25,000 debt that I owed my brother.

At the 1993 Chicago Partners' Seminar, God spoke to me to give another $1,000. I asked God to set me free from the bondage of credit cards. All of a sudden I had people coming in at the station to sell me their cars. I bought their cars, fixed them up, and sold them. I knew it was God. In two weeks I sold six cars – making huge profits on each of them – and was able to pay off all my credit card debts.

At the World Conference in 1994, I gave $300 to Operation Israel. Two months later I received a letter from Home Savings saying that my monthly home payments would be reduced by $400 a month. I wasn't expecting this and it was a real blessing to me.

God also blessed me with two new cars. We now send our children to private school. Everything we touch turns into a blessing. The blessings are still continuing and I am able to be a blessing to others."

> The blessings are still continuing and I am able to be a blessing to others

Ganga Ramnaraine

"During Morris Cerullo's 1993 Florida World Conference, I felt that I should give $2,000 (£1,250) in the offering.

While I was at the Conference, a call came from my

family that my two-year old grandson, Roy, was in hospital. Later the doctor told me that Roy had a malignant brain tumor and they would have to operate. I called and asked Dr Cerullo to pray for Roy. He came through the operation wonderfully and was standing up in bed within half an hour.

Before we brought Roy home from hospital, they told my son the bill was $67,000 (£41,875). My son's insurance had expired three months before the operation and he did not know about it. The company was not going to pay his bill.

My son talked with the doctor and he said, 'We're going to take care of it. You don't bother. Take your son and go home!' The whole debt of $67,000 was canceled! This entire testimony took place just after I obeyed God and gave sacrificially for the first time."

Rebecca Hager

"In 1972, I discovered that the Bureau of Land management had never released 135 acres of Mountain Vacant land which I had bought and paid for. For ten years Dr Cerullo stood in agreement with me for the release of this property.

In 1982, God reminded me of a vow to MCWE of $100 for Israel. I paid this and again requested prayer that the land be released. This time it happened.

At the 1992 Elders' meeting in San Diego, Dr Cerullo prophesied that the real estate which we had held for a long period of time would be sold. Within five days of returning home, I had a contract to sell one plot of this land for $120,000 (£75,000) cash. Three months later another plot sold for $95,000 (£59,375) cash. Six months later another plot sold for $200,000 (£125,000). I was holding deeds of trust for $100,000 (£625,00), and unexpectedly this was also paid in cash.

This makes a total of $525,000 (£328,125) cash in 1992. Out of this I was able to give over $30,000 into foreign missions. I invested in more real estate, bought a new car, paid off the second mortgage on my daughter's home, remodeled my home, and went to the Ukraine. I planted a church west of Kiev by holding a three day crusade. I rented a building and paid two pastors' salaries for six months in advance.

I now have a contract with the television station in Rivine, 300 miles west of Moscow. I pay for a television program which is reaching about two and a half million people daily."

Paul Lubega

"In 1993 I went from my home in Sweden to Morris Cerullo's World Conference in Florida. At that time I had a large tax debt due, but I placed $1,000 in the offering for the Billion Soul Crusade vision given to Dr Cerullo by God. I also gave for the Jewish Outreach. I gave a deposit at the conference and sent the balance when I returned home.

We feel that God gave us these businesses as a result of our sacrificial giving

Immediately, God began to open doors. He gave my wife and I two new businesses. One was a department store, the other was a small restaurant.

We did not have the money to purchase these businesses, but through supernatural intervention God provided the money. We feel that God gave us these businesses as a result of our sacrificial giving at the World Conference.

God also blessed us by allowing us to purchase a plot of ground in Uganda, our home of origin, for a very small price. God has provided to such an extent, that we have no lack or struggle."

Raphael Barnado

"I live in Togo, Africa, and have been very greatly blessed by Morris Cerullo's ministry.

When I came to the United States in 1993 for the World Conference, God did a work inside me. He spoke to me during one of the services and he told me to start supporting his ministry. I gave $2,700 (£1,687).

Upon my return to Togo, miracles began breaking forth. Among them, a high-ranking country official invited me to pray for him. This person was blessed and gave me money. He did this three times and I received a total of $10,000."

Valnice Milhomons

Valnice Milhomons is a great woman evangelist and teacher in Brazil. In January 1993, she attended Morris Cerullo's annual World Conference.

While there, she felt God move upon her as she heard Dr Cerullo share about the Jewish Outreach. In obedience to God, she gave $5,000 (£3,125) for the Jews.

The money she gave was her personal savings which she had amassed over a period of forty years.

Four months after this, God gave her a wonderful house in Brazil. The house is for her ministry headquarters and is valued at $500,000. This new HQ for Valnice's ministry was dedicated in September 1993 for the Glory of God.

Darlene Anthens

"Ever since I attended an MCWE School of Ministry in California in May 1988, my life has been revolutionized. It keeps on getting better and better as blessing after blessing continues to come upon me.

At the beginning of January 1994, I gave $1,000 for Operation Israel. I love to give to the Jews. God has put a real burden on my heart for them.

> I love to give to the Jews. God has put a real burden on my heart for them

I joined the forty-day fast in February 1994. One of my prayer requests was for a debt cancellation of $26,000 (£16,250). I agreed to covenant in prayer and fasting for forty days – and the debt cancellation was one of the agreements for my prayer to be answered. I began to take each of the steps that Dr Cerullo requested, giving $100, $200 and so on.

A week later, I received a letter from Dr Cerullo which asked me to give towards a ministry airplane.

I gave $5,000 for the airplane. Shortly after this my uncle died, and his wife died six days later. I received $334,000 from their estate and was able to pay off my debts.

This was totally unexpected. Their will had stipulated that whatever was left over in their estate would go to the other one, and that if both of them expired, everything should come to me.

Since the beginning of 1994, God has enabled me to give over $7,000 (£4,375) to MCWE. That's coming from behind because I started giving with nothing."

> I received $334,000 from their estate and was able to pay off my debts. This was totally unexpected

Sandra Bell

"I attended Morris Cerullo's 1989 World Conference after going through a series of financial troubles which were the result of a divorce. Everyone knew I was going under. The question was, 'How would I survive as a single parent?'

At the World Conference, Morris Cerullo made a

statement about the blessing of God running after those who made a sacrificial gift towards the work of God.

I made a vow for $1,000 and placed the $2 I had in the envelope. When I returned home, I unexpectedly received a cheque for $998 which was exactly what I needed to fulfill the vow I'd made during the Conference. Immediately, I sent the money to MCWE.

As a direct result, I believe, of my faithfulness to God, I received a financial blessing in my job with a salary increase of $10,000. I am the head nurse of a dialysis program at the Lutheran Medical Center in Brooklyn.

I praise God for his faithfulness. He has performed financial miracles for me over and over again."

Louise Piche

"During MCWE's forty day feast in 1994, I vowed to give $500. I was at Dr Cerullo's meeting in Toronto without any money, so I trusted God to supply the gift. He did. I received a $1,000 bonus from my employers because of my work and commitment to the company.

This was a miracle because the company was not doing well financially. I could pay my vow with no problem!

> My $500 gift was part of a memorial prayer that I am lifting up to God

My $500 (£312) gift was part of a memorial prayer that I am lifting up to God, asking him to help me breakthrough in intercessory prayer. Like Hannah in the Bible, I am pouring out my soul to God and must have a breakthrough.

I am blessed to be one of Dr Cerullo's partners. God has us working together to accomplish his perfect plan to reach the nations of the world for his glory."

Onesmo Mwakyambo

In 1986, Onesmo attended Morris Cerullo's All African Congress on Evangelism, where he learned about getting a breakthrough in his finances.

At this Congress he did not have any money to give in the offering, but he was wearing two shirts. He took one of them and placed this in the offering.

Onesmo went back to his church and taught a seminar on finances. Everyone was to give their best offering and tell God how they wanted to be blessed. Onesmo's wife asked God for a vehicle. Soon they were given a Toyota Truck.

> He did not have any money to give in the offering, but he was wearing two shirts. So he took one of them and placed it in the offering

In 1987, God gave Onesmo some land for a give-away price of $100.

He planted rice. In six months he had made $222,000 (£138,750), more than double the amount normally received for his crop.

God told Onesmo to give the total amount to his church for a sound system. He planted another crop. In six months Onesmo made $250,000 (£156,250). He gave his tithe, plus half of his income to God's work.

Onesmo bought more land. In six months, during high inflation, he received $80,000 (£50,000), which would have been three times higher if there had not been inflation.

Onesmo asked God for more land so that he could provide for the ministry. In 1993, a man who wouldn't sell to anyone else gave Onesmo twenty acres for the best price. Onesmo also bought other land around him, and now has 200 acres of sugar and rice plantations.

Onesmo also conducts seminars and Schools of Ministry in evangelism as well as a School of Ministry for children in

the secondary schools. He continues to give his tithe, plus
half his total income to God.

Carolyn & Michael Wallace

"I attended MCWE's 1993 World Conference and gave to
the Jewish World Outreach by making a pledge of $100,
which I paid when I returned home.

God also told me to give $100 every month to support
Morris Cerullo's ministry. God said that this was good,
fertile and moist soil because the Holy Spirit had ordained
the ministry. The Word of God is being preached with signs
and wonders following.

My husband and I didn't have any money to give. We
had three mortgages on our homes and business, and owed
the IRS $5,000 (£3,125).

During the time God told us to give, my husband said
'Look, we don't have any money. You are giving $100 and
we don't have any food money.' I said, 'God said it, I know
he will do it'.

**We took hold of giving
and continued to give
every time that we could**

We also went to the 1993
Chicago Partners' Seminar.
We made a pledge of $1,300
(£812) and paid this pledge as
soon as we came home. We took hold of giving and
continued to give every time that we could.

The IRS ended up owing us 1,200 (£750). The $5,000 we
owed them was canceled. We owed back rent to two
landlords on our businesses – one landlord wrote off our
debt of $18,000 (£11,250) and the other landlord wrote off
another debt of $13,000 (£8,125) – we only had to pay
$2,000. We are completely out of debt.

At a 1994 meeting, Morris Cerullo shared a testimony of
a man who said, 'We give....to get....to give.'

We had to get out of debt – and then we got back to

scratch and started building up again in our business. Now we can say, 'We've got it. We give to get to give.'"

Joseph Parnell

"From 1976 to 1988, I owned seven Burger Kings and one Steak House. Because of my divorce, I lost all of it except for the Steak House.

In 1989, I came to the World Conference and gave $11,000 to the Jewish Outreach – exactly the amount I owed the seller of the Steak House.

I also owed the bank $500,000 (£343,750). At the January 1993 Conference I gave $1,000 to the Jewish Outreach. The bank canceled the $500,000 I owed to them.

In January 1993 I gave $1,000 to the Jewish Outreach, and the bank canceled the $500,000 I owed to them

Then the man I owed money for the Steak house made the loss over to a bank which promptly went bankrupt. My $11,000 debt – along with the interest which raised it to $20,000 – disappeared.

In September 1993, after the twenty-one day fast, the court ruled in my favor in a tax court case – canceling $200,000 to the IRS which had arisen from my divorce.

As of December 31 1994, I am debt free and am now praying for the restoration of my family."

Janet Stalb

"In October 1992, I received a prophecy letter from Morris Cerullo stating that God was going to cancel his children's debts by the end of 1992. It was for whoever heard the prophecy and acted on it.

At first I was reluctant to believe because we've been deceived by other televangelists. But this scripture kept coming to me. 'When a prophet speaks in the name of the

Lord, if the thing follow not, nor come to pass, that is the thing which the Lord has not spoken, but the prophet has spoken it presumptuously: you shall not be afraid of him.' (Deuteronomy 18:22.)

I took a step of faith and sent Dr Cerullo's ministry a cheque for $40 (£25). Just twenty days later, my father-in-law called, requesting to see my husband.

My husband went to see him and when he returned he had a cheque made out in the amount of $10,000 (£6,250)!

We are out of debt and no longer striving to make ends meet! I pray that many others will act upon the prophecy which was proclaimed. What God does for one, he will do for others!

> I took a step of faith and sent Dr Cerullo's ministry a cheque for $40

I worried about our finances because we had been struggling for fourteen years. I was not trusting God fully in the area of finances. The Holy Spirit gave me courage to step out and act upon the prophecy given through Morris Cerullo. I praise God!"

GREAT ENCOURAGEMENT

I trust that these testimonies have been an enormous encouragement to us all. Certainly, I never fail to be awed by God's power and love when my partners describe how he has met their needs in such miraculous ways.

We serve the all-giving God who delights to honor his word and fulfill his promises. What he says does come true. When we follow his giving principles, we can rely on him completely to supply all our needs.

The people we've read about in this chapter are ordinary people who took a step of faith for many different reasons. Some gave in thanks; others gave because of their love; a few gave to have their own needs met. And God dealt with them according to all the promises we've noted in the Bible.

These partners of mine are givers who became receivers; they are people who've found that the secret of receiving is giving by faith. There is absolutely no reason why every single reader of this book should not experience exactly the same level of overflowing blessing. However large our needs may seem to us, we know that they are not beyond the resources of Almighty God.

I promise that when we give like these partners we will receive like them too. May these testimonies act not just as a monument to God's grace, but also as a spur which prompts us all to start giving generously in faith and obedience.

A GIVING PARTNERSHIP

This has been a hard book to write. Who could possibly write about such a subject without being aware of their own shortcomings! But it has also been a wonderful book to write, for the joy and blessing of giving and receiving have impressed themselves upon me in a fresh way.

Sometimes critics have accused me of asking people to give for our ministry's sake. It's true that there's a job to be done which needs financing, but how much more I long for us all to experience the delight of generous Scriptural giving – which results in us receiving so many wonderful blessings here on earth.

Yet more than that, I don't want anyone to be disappointed on the great day which is before us all. I don't want a single partner to be ignorant of how they can receive a great eternal reward from God. I don't want anybody to ask why I hadn't explained to them about converting earthly wealth into heavenly currency. And I want everybody to discover that the secret of receiving is giving by faith.

We're going to spend eternity worshipping God with all our wonderful Jewish and Third World brothers and sisters. I know that I'm incredibly privileged in being able to meet them and worship with them here on earth. I sincerely hope that – as a direct result of the change in the way we all give – this book will make a practical difference to their lives.

As you now arrive at the last page – before you put the book down – I want you to stop and consider what changes you should make in your giving patterns.

This book will have been written in vain if it doesn't revolutionize the way that we all think about giving, doesn't transform our actual giving, and doesn't trigger an avalanche of divine blessing into our lives.

Please reflect on what I've written, and promise to put into practice all the different things that God has pressed upon you.

Finally, it may be that God has blessed you through this ministry – perhaps through this book – and you now want to stand with me as a partner. Please write to me. My address is over the page. It will be a deep honor to share with you in the work of the gospel.

For more information on this worldwide ministry,
please write to:

Morris Cerullo World Evangelism

PO Box 85277
San Diego
CA 92186
USA

PO Box 277
Hemel Hempstead
Herts HP2 7DA
Britain

PO Box 3600
Concord
Ontario L4K 1B6
Canada